INSPIRED BY
THE
PASSION
TRANSLATION

Grace
and *Hope*

A 40-DAY DEVOTIONAL FOR
LENT AND EASTER

tPt

Dr. Brian Simmons

BroadStreet
PUBLISHING

Grace and Hope

A 40-Day Devotional for Lent and Easter

By Dr. Brian Simmons with Jeremy Bouma

© 2016 BroadStreet Publishing Group

Inspired by *The Passion Translation* by Dr. Brian Simmons
ThePassionTranslation.com

Published by BroadStreet Publishing Group, LLC
Racine, Wisconsin, USA
BroadStreetPublishing.com

ISBN-13: 978-1-4245-5191-0 (hard cover)
ISBN-13: 978-1-4245-5070-8 (e-book)

Cover design by Garborg Design Works, Inc. www.garborgdesign.com
Interior design and typesetting by Katherine Lloyd at www.TheDESKonline.com

Printed in China
16 17 18 19 20 5 4 3 2 1

Contents

INTRODUCTION

"Remember that you are dust, and to dust you will return."

So begins the yearly Christian season known as Lent, a follow-up of sorts to the season of Advent.

While during Advent we celebrate the various "comings" of Christ—first as a baby born to take away the sins of the world, and second as the victorious king come again to put the world to rights—during Lent we traditionally take a more contemplative posture, examining ourselves and our own mortality in order to personally identify with what Christ did to break our chains of sin.

In the book of Hebrews we find the perfect marriage of these two important Christian seasons:

Since all his "children" have flesh and blood, so Jesus became human to fully identify with us. He did this, so that he could experience death and annihilate the effects of the intimidating accuser, who holds against us the power of death. By embracing death Jesus sets free those who live their entire lives in bondage to the tormenting dread of death (Hebrews 2:14–15).

Consider this: Jesus became one of us and lived our life

in order to experience our death, so that he could break the power of death reflected in the opening words above! This is what we reflect upon and celebrate during the season of Lent.

For those who are unfamiliar with Lent, it is a forty-day journey of self-reflection and self-denial that prepares the believer for Holy Week, leading to Good Friday and Resurrection Sunday. Throughout this period Christians are invited to examine themselves as they remember the suffering and sacrifice of Jesus on their behalf. It's also a time for setting aside our past sins and failures in light of the blessed future hope of who we will become by God's grace. Accompanying this season of repentance is fasting, almsgiving, reflection, and prayer.

Lent officially begins with Ash Wednesday, a solemn service in which we're called to remember our mortality and express our need for God's mercy and forgiveness. We are invited to remember that one day we will return to the dust from whence we came, and it is by God's gracious gift that we will be resurrected from the dead and given everlasting life.

Traditionally, this season has been marked by fasting from food and entertainment as a way to experience, in some way, Christ's own self-denial. You may have known a friend or coworker who gave up chocolate or Facebook, wine or TV—perhaps you yourself fasted from something or some experience for Lent as a way to prepare for Easter. While it may sound silly, these forty days of self-denial are meant to help believers identify with and understand the depths of Christ's own self-denial on our behalf through his suffering and sacrifice on the cross.

But why forty days? The number "forty" is deeply scriptural: God sent rain for forty days and nights during the great Noah flood; Moses spent forty days on Mt. Sinai with God; the children of Israel wandered in the wilderness for forty years before gaining the Promised Land; and Jesus went into his own wilderness and fasted for forty days, where he was tested and tempted by Satan before he began his ministry.

So it is this deep, biblical history that inspired early Christians to begin setting aside these days to focus the heart and prepare the soul to celebrate the most important events in history: the death and resurrection of Jesus Christ. And it is this practice that inspired this Lenten devotional using a faithful and fresh, reliable and relevant new translation of the Bible, *The Passion Translation*.

The goal of *The Passion Translation* is to reintroduce the passion and fire of the Bible to the English reader. It doesn't merely convey the original, literal meaning of words. It expresses God's passion for people and his world by translating the original, life-changing message of God's Word for modern readers.

God longs to have his Word expressed in every language in a way that would unlock the passion of his heart. Our goal is to trigger inside every English speaker an overwhelming response to the truth of the Bible. This is a heart-level translation, from the passion of God's heart to the passion of your heart. And we've put this devotional together to help introduce you to it in a way that will bless your walk through the Lenten and Easter seasons.

For each of the forty days Lent is observed, Monday through Saturday, we have selected a meaningful passage of Scripture for meditation. You'll also find a short devotion based on that day's reading and a special Lenten prayer to help guide you through this holy season of self-reflection and self-denial, prayer and fasting, repentance and remembrance—all to prepare you for the hopeful words, "It is finished!" and the even more wondrous words, "He is risen!"

We trust this version of God's Word will kindle in you a burning, passionate desire for him and his heart, while impacting the church for years to come. We also pray this Lenten devotional will encourage and inspire your faith in the One who bore our pain and shame, so that you could be declared "Not guilty!" and enjoy everlasting life in the age to come!

Day 1

Psalm 51:1–14

1-2God, give me mercy from your fountain of forgiveness!
  I know your abundant love is enough
  to wash away my guilt.
  Because your compassion is so great,
  take away this shameful guilt of sin.
  Forgive the full extent of my rebellious ways,
  and erase this deep stain on my conscience.
3-4For I'm so ashamed.
  I feel such pain and anguish within me
  I can't get away from the sting of my sin against you, Lord!
  Everything I did, I did right in front of you, for you saw it all.
  Against you, and you above all, have I sinned.
  Everything you say to me is infallibly true
  and your judgment conquers me.
5Lord, I have been a sinner from birth.
  Sin's corruption has polluted my soul.
6I know that you delight to set your truth deep in my spirit.
  So come into the hidden places of my heart
  and teach me wisdom.
7Purify my conscience! Make this leper clean again!
  Wash me in your love until I am pure in heart.

⁸Satisfy me in your sweetness, and my song of joy will return.
> The places within me you have crushed
> will rejoice in your healing touch.

⁹Hide my sins from your face;
> erase all my guilt by your saving grace.

¹⁰Create a new, clean heart within me.
> Fill me with pure thoughts and holy desires,
> ready to please you.

¹¹May you never reject me!
> May you never take from me your Sacred Spirit!

¹²Let my passion for life be restored,
> tasting joy in every breakthrough you bring to me.
> Hold me close to you with a willing spirit
> that obeys whatever you say.

¹³Then I can show to other guilty ones
> how loving and merciful you are.
> They will find their way back home to you,
> knowing that you will forgive them.

¹⁴O God, my saving God,
> deliver me fully from every sin,
> even the sin that brought blood-guilt to my soul.
> Then my heart will once again be thrilled to sing
> the passionate songs of joy and deliverance!

The Overflowing Fountain
of God's Grace!

*O*ne day you are going to die.

On that day your heart will stop, your organs will shut down. Later you'll be lowered into a six-foot hole in the ground, and eventually your flesh will decompose into dust.

Sobering, isn't it?

Yet, this is the way Christians have opened the Lenten season, leading to celebrating the most wondrous events in the history of the world: the death and resurrection of Jesus Christ.

If you've attended an Ash Wednesday service, you know the drill: after the service's reading and sermon, you kneel before the minister to receive the sign of the cross upon your forehead, made with the ashes of burnt palm fronds from the previous year's Palm Sunday service. And then you hear these words, reminding you of your mortality:

"Remember you are dust, and to dust you will return."

Why do you suppose the church launches this season in this way? Why contemplate our death on the road to celebrating Christ's death?

I think I know the answer: Until you grasp the gravity of the consequence of sin against God, you can't fully appreciate the gift of Christ's defeat of it. Paul reminds us of this consequence in Romans 6:23: "For sin's meager wages is death."

The wage we earn because of our work of rebellion against God is death. That is our ultimate problem, requiring the ultimate fix—which, of course, we contemplate and celebrate at the end of our Lenten journey.

Perhaps it's why after the imposition of ashes we are invited to read or sing Psalm 51. If you haven't read it yet, do so now. While there's a lot to celebrate, there's also a lot to mourn, because the condition this poet describes is the condition we all share.

Notice how the psalmist feels about his condition. It is "shameful." It's a "deep stain" on his conscience. He is "ashamed." It stings. He feels "pain and anguish" because of it, and his soul has been "polluted" by sin's corruption.

Perhaps you can relate to this feeling of shame and anguish, this sting and pain. I know I can. While it can be uncomfortable and not a little depressing to think about our sin, we must at some point come to grips with it; that is part of the reason we enter into and engage Lent, after all.

And yet…we are not without hope! For as the psalmist reveals, God has a "fountain of forgiveness" bursting with grace for every single person on the planet!

Including you, brother; including you, sister!

God longs to purify each of us and make us clean again; he longs to wash us until we are pure again.

The beauty and majesty of the Lenten and Easter season

is that the grace of God flows freely to those who confess their sins and seek God's healing touch. In fact, an old hymn speaks of this fountain:

> There is a fountain filled with blood
> Drawn from Immanuel's veins;
> And sinners, plunged beneath that flood,
> Lose all their guilty stains:
> Lose all their guilty stains,
> Lose all their guilty stains;
> And sinners, plunged beneath that flood,
> Lose all their guilty stains.*

Brother, sister, over the next forty days remember that you are dust, and to dust you will return. But also remember there is a fountain of forgiveness out of which flows the magnificent, matchless grace of God to cleanse and purify your guilty stains!

Lenten Prayer

Heavenly Father, at the beginning of Lent I confess all of my rebellious acts against you and your name, and I echo the prayer of the psalmist: Purify my conscience! Make this leper clean again! Wash me in

---

* William Cowper, "There is a Fountain Filled with Blood," Public Domain, pub. 1772.

your love until I am pure in heart. Satisfy me in your sweetness, and my song of joy will return. Hide my sins from your face; erase all my guilt in your saving grace. Start over with me, and create a new, clean heart within me!

Day 2

John 1:14–17

¹⁴And so the Living Expression
became a man and lived among us!
And we gazed upon the splendor of his glory,
the glory of the One and Only
who came from the Father overflowing
with tender mercy and truth!
¹⁵John taught the truth about him
when he announced to the people,
"He's the One! *Set your hearts on him!*
I told you he would come after me,
even though he ranks far above me,
for he existed before I was even born."
¹⁶And now out of his fullness we are fulfilled!
And from him we receive grace heaped
upon more grace!
¹⁷Moses gave us the Law, but Jesus, the Anointed One,
unveils truth wrapped in tender mercy.

He's the One;
Set Your Hearts on Him!

$\mathcal{L}$ ife is lived waiting, isn't it?

You sit at a stoplight, waiting for it to turn green. You wait in line to order your lunch or dinner. You wait for that package to arrive.

You wait for the results on the plastic stick, either one line or two. And then you wait for the baby to be born and grow up—and (hopefully) move out of the house!

You wait for Mr. or Ms. Right or that promised job promotion.

Life is lived waiting.

Now imagine waiting for the one promised to come restore your nation to its former glory, by defeating the foreign invaders; driving them from the land; turning the nation around morally; and reestablishing religious order.

That's what Israel had been waiting for for generation upon generation: they were waiting for the Messiah, the Anointed One.

During the time of Jesus, the Jewish people were waiting for the One who would come riding on a horse to fight their final fight, rescue their nation by driving Rome from their land, and put them back together again through Torah observance and temple worship.

And yet when Jesus came, the gospel of John tells us that he wasn't recognized or received—even by his own people!

But John the Baptizer did. He had taught people for years about the coming salvation from Yahweh and invited them to repent for the forgiveness of their sins—just like his father Zechariah prophesied at his birth. (See Luke 1:76–79.)

Then one day—there he was!

Jesus came walking toward John and he let all the world know that *this* was the One they had been waiting for for generations!

Do you know that Jesus is who you've been waiting for, too? That he is the One promised from long ago who would come to fight your final fight, rescue your life, and put your life back together again?

John says Jesus came bearing the very things we've needed all along:

Grace and truth.

Jesus brought truth-filled grace, or grace-wrapped truth—however you look at it.

Jesus tells the truth about who we are: brilliantly crafted statues of God who have been created in his image. Yet sin marred God's image in these statues so they needed to be recreated.

Yet right alongside that truth is grace—God's unmerited, unworked-for favor and love. John tells us that those who embrace Jesus and take hold of his name are given authority to become who they really are—children of God! Grace heaped upon more grace beckons us and establishes us in God's family, as full heirs of his glorious riches! God's grace and love make us a new creation in Christ, in the process of being conformed to his image again.

During Lent we need both grace and truth. We need to be reminded who we *were* as sinners and reminded who we *are* as children. We need to contemplate the truth of our past (and, perhaps, present) mistakes, while receiving heaps of God's love, allowing that contrast to birth thankfulness in our hearts that rises in worship to our Savior.

He is the one you've been waiting for; now set your heart on him and him alone!

Lenten Prayer

Jesus, I recognize you are the One I've been waiting for my whole life to rescue me from sin and death and restore me to the way you intended me to be. I confess I don't always treat you that way, but this day I vow to set my heart on you and you alone! Amen.

Day 3

John 1:29–34

²⁹The very next day John saw Jesus coming to him to be baptized, and John cried out, "Look! There he is—God's Lamb! He will take away the sins of the world! ³⁰I told you that a Mighty One would come who is far greater than I am, because he existed long before I was born! ³¹My baptism was for the preparation of his appearing to Israel, even though I've yet to experience him."

³²Then, as John baptized Jesus he spoke these words: "I see the Spirit of God appear like a dove descending from the heavenly realm and landing upon him—and it rested upon him from that moment forward! ³³And even though I've yet to experience him, when I was commissioned to baptize with water God spoke these words to me, 'One day you will see the Spirit descend and remain upon a man. He will be the One I have sent to baptize with the Holy Spirit.' ³⁴And now I have seen with discernment. I can tell you for sure that this man is the Son of God."

Look, the Lamb of God!

*H*ave you ever wondered why John called Jesus "the *Lamb* of God"? Sounds like an odd title. The *Son* of God makes sense. So do Prince of Peace, Emmanuel, the Messiah, and others. Why Lamb?

To understand this significant title we need to go way back into the story of Israel, because this name is deeply Jewish.

Remember the story of the exodus? This story tells of the day when God rescued his people from the hands of the Egyptians using his servant Moses. Because Pharaoh's heart was hardened to God's command to "let [his] people go!" God sent a series of plagues. Yet frogs and locusts, boils and darkness couldn't turn his heart. It was only after God sent the plague that killed each firstborn that Pharaoh finally relented.

This plague was the most devastating of them all, for after midnight God swept over the whole land of Egypt, taking the life of the firstborn son of every person—from Pharaoh to slaves to cattle.

But not the Israelites. The Lord provided protection in the form of a lamb.

It was called the *Passover lamb*.

He told his people to slaughter it and smear its blood on the top and on both sides of the doorframe of their home. When the Lord came, he would see the blood, pass over the home, and not destroy their firstborn. And he did! He spared the lives of his faithful ones—all because the blood of that *pass over* lamb.

Passover is celebrated to this day. It was celebrated in Jesus' day, too—the day he was slaughtered for the sins of the world.

Yet instead of smearing blood over the wood of the doorposts of a home, his blood dripped from the wood of a Roman cross. It is that blood that has taken away the sins of the world!

And here is John, making the announcement to all who would listen the *ultimate* Passover lamb had arrived to spare the lives of his faithful ones. From the very beginning of Jesus' story we have a glimpse of his fateful end: a slaughtered lamb, *God's* slaughtered Lamb.

Through this sacrifice, Jesus not only dealt with the *fruit* of the world's sins but the *root*, too. Jesus solved the problem of both the *effects* of our rebellion and its *cause*, both the *results* and *source* of our foul deeds.

And check this out: Our sins are *removed*! Taken away! Vanished—*poof*!

Look at how the psalmist describes this removal:

Farther than from a sunrise to a sunset;
that's how far you've removed our guilt from us!
(Psalm 103:12)

I love this metaphor, because there is no end to the length between the east and the west; its distance is infinite!

That's how far God has removed the fruit and root of your sin, your sin guilt and sin nature!

Because Jesus, the Lamb of God, willingly crawled up on the butcher's block of the cross, God no longer sees your sin when he looks at you. Instead, he sees a lovely, lovable son or daughter!

John's name for Jesus takes on a whole new meaning, doesn't it?

That's who Jesus is: He is the Lamb of God, who took away your sins and the sins of the world!

Lenten Prayer

Jesus Christ, Lamb of God, I praise you and thank you for shedding your blood upon the Roman cross so that God's judgment would pass over me! Amen.

Day 4

John 1:35–42

[35-36] The very next day John was there again with two of his disciples as Jesus was walking right past them. John, gazing upon him, pointed to Jesus and said, "Look! There's God's Lamb!" [37] And as soon as John's two disciples heard this, they immediately left John and began to follow a short distance behind Jesus.

[38] Then Jesus turned around and saw they were following him and asked, "What do you want?" They responded, "Rabbi (which means, Master Teacher), where are you staying?" [39] Jesus answered, "Come and discover for yourselves." So they went with him and saw where he was staying, and since it was late in the afternoon, they spent the rest of the day with Jesus.

[40-41] One of the two disciples who heard John's words and began to follow Jesus was a man named Andrew. He went and found his brother, Simon, and told him, "We have found the Anointed One!" (Which is translated, the Christ.) [42] Then Andrew brought Simon to meet him. When Jesus gazed upon Andrew's brother, he prophesied to him, "You are Simon and your father's name is John. But from now on you will be called Cephas" (which means, Peter the Rock).

What Do You Want?

*T*hese are the first words Jesus speaks in John's gospel: "Hey, fellas, what are you looking for? What do you want?"

How simple, yet how profound!

These aren't the first questions you'd expect coming from the so-called "Son of God," are they?

Yet it makes sense, considering why Jesus came in the first place: to bridge the gap between sinful humans and a holy God.

It's as if he is reaching into the deepest longings of these two people and inviting them to share what it is that only he can fulfill and repair after our ancient ancestors, Adam and Eve, created a God-shaped hole in all of us.

You know, this question is very similar to another question God himself asked. This one takes us all the way back to the very beginning of the story—as in Genesis beginning.

In Genesis 3 we find our second question shortly after Adam and Eve rebelled against God by eating from the Tree of Knowledge of Good and Evil. After their eyes were opened, they hid themselves—trying to cover their shame and guilt all on their own.

Shortly thereafter, God comes calling for his beloved creatures. Yet, rather than summon them for rebuke, he searches for them for relationship—armed with our second simple, profound question:

"Where are you?"

These two people separated themselves from God by demanding to live life on their own terms. And it brought them nothing but shame and guilt, anxiety and alienation.

We've been doing and experiencing the same ever since. And like Adam and Eve, we've been trying to fix our problem, which is why Jesus' question is so profound—and important.

Because, you see, Jesus is who these two men had been waiting for their whole lives! And just as God the Father invited Adam and Eve to come out from hiding and into the light of fellowship, Jesus does the same. God the Son invites these seekers to "come and discover" for themselves who Jesus is and what Jesus offers.

They won't fully understand what it is he means for them—and the world—until the end, when Christ offers himself as a sacrifice unto suffering and death. But along the way they see for themselves how Jesus can answer his simple, profound three-word question:

The lame are healed, the blind see, the dead are raised back to new life, and the good news of God's grace-filled kingdom realm is spread far and wide!

Yet even from the beginning they get how Jesus is the answer to his own question. Because after they "saw where he was staying" and "spent the rest of the day with" him, these two just knew! They knew Jesus was who they'd been waiting for their whole lives, because one of the men, Andrew, runs off to find his brother, Simon Peter. What does he tell him?

"Simon, Simon! We've found him! We have found the Anointed One, the Christ!"

And then Simon, whom Jesus names Peter the Rock, comes and discovers what his brother had seen.

The same questions Jesus asked of Andrew and his friend he is asking every single person on the planet: "What do you want? What are you looking for?"

It's a question only he can ask, because it's an answer only he can give.

Lenten Prayer

Jesus, I am reminded this day that you are who I have been waiting for my whole life: my Savior and Redeemer, my Shelter and Shield, my Rescuer and Restorer. I thank you and praise your name for all that you've done and all you are for me! Amen.

Day 5

Psalm 80:1-7

¹God-Enthroned, be revealed in splendor
   as you ride upon the cherubim!
   How perfectly you lead us, a people set free.
   Loving Shepherd of Israel—listen to our hearts' cry!
   Shine forth from your throne of dazzling light.
²In the sight of Benjamin, Ephraim, and Manasseh,
   stir up your mighty power in full display before our eyes.
   Breakthrough and reveal yourself
      by coming to our rescue.
³Revive us, O God! Let your beaming face shine upon us
   with the sunrise rays of glory;
   then nothing will be able to stop us.
⁴O God, the Mighty Commander of Angel-Armies,
   how much longer will you smolder in anger?
   How much longer will you be disgusted with your people
   even when they pray?
⁵You have fed us with sorrow and grief
   and made us drink our tears by the bowlful.
⁶You've made us a thorn in the side of
      all the neighboring lands,
   and now they just laugh at us with their mocking scorn.

7Come back, come back, O God, and restore us!
>   You are the Commander of Angel-Armies.
>   Let your beaming face shine upon us
>   with the sunrise rays of glory,
>   and then nothing will be able to stop us!

Come Back and Revive Me, God!

We ended the first few days of Lent by reflecting on the beginning of our human story, when Adam and Eve brought death to mankind and all of creation after rebelling against God. We looked at one of the most important questions God ever asked humanity—"Where are you?" There's something else we need to notice about this unexpected twist in our story, though:

God came back!

Have you ever noticed this about the so-called "fall" story of Adam and Eve? Maybe it's overlooked because it's so obvious, but think about it:

God's precious creatures, the pinnacle of his creative endeavor, the ones who were molded and crafted in his image and likeness rebelled. They turned their backs on him! They said, "God, we don't want to live *that* way, we want to live *this* way—we *insist* on living this way, as self-made gods."

How would you react if someone you loved—a friend, your spouse, your child—turned their back on you and said, "Thanks, but no thanks" to a relationship with you?

I'd probably say, "Thanks, but no thanks" myself and leave them in the dust!

Not God. No, instead he came back! To pursue them, to rescue them, to revive them.

You know what? He's been doing the same ever since!

Psalm 80 reminds us that God comes back and rescues and revives. This song was a prayer of lament members of the tribes of Judah prayed. They were in decline, they were in trouble, they had been rejected by God because of willful rebellion against him.

Sounds familiar, doesn't it?

And so the people of God got on their knees and sung or said this psalm as a prayer asking the "Loving Shepherd of Israel [to] listen to [their] hearts' cry!"

They wanted him to "stir up [his] mighty power" and "break through and reveal [himself] by coming to [their] rescue." They longed for God to "revive" them, to let his "beaming face shine upon [them] with the sunrise rays of glory."

Perhaps, more importantly, they wondered, "How much longer will you smolder in anger? How much longer will you be disgusted with your people even when they pray?"

Have you ever wondered the same, after realizing and recognizing your sin, or after experiencing sin's consequences, like Israel?

The list of Israel's rebellious acts against God was long and ongoing: idolatry, witchcraft, pagan rituals, pagan sexual practices, and on and on.

No wonder God seemed so distant as the fallout of their sin kept increasing!

And no wonder Israel prayed that he would come back and revive them!

This same song and prayer was probably on the lips of Jews living in Palestine under Roman occupation two thousand years ago, too.

They were in decline, they were in trouble, they hadn't heard from God in nearly four centuries, and they were waiting for the Anointed One—the "Branch-Man, the Son of your love, the Son of Man who dwells at your right hand," as the psalmist goes on to say (Psalm 80:17).

God promised this One would come to save them, rescue them, and revive them—the same promise given to you and me and the entire world all the way back in Genesis 3!

When God came back to his beloved creatures, God promised he would send One who would crush the serpent's head, after the serpent struck his heal.

Jesus was that One! Jesus shows us that God made good on his promise to come back and rescue and revive the crowning achievement of his creation. He did so by becoming one of us and being "struck"—through shame, suffering, and the ultimate sacrifice: death.

Remember that this Lenten season, that God *did* come back—for you, for Israel, for the world—bearing rescue, revival, and restoration!

Lenten Prayer

Heavenly Father, thank you for not giving up on us when we rebelled against you in the garden. Thank you for not giving up on me, either! Amen.

Day 6

Hebrews 2:14–18

[14]Since all his "children" have flesh and blood, so Jesus became human to fully identify with us. He did this, so that he could experience death and annihilate the effects of the intimidating accuser who holds against us the power of death. [15]By embracing death Jesus sets free those who live their entire lives in bondage to the tormenting dread of death. [16]For it is clear that he didn't do this for the angels, but for all the sons and daughters of Abraham. [17]This is why he had to be a Man and take hold of our humanity in every way. He made us his brothers and sisters and became our merciful and faithful King-Priest before God, as the One who removed our sins to make us one with him. [18]He suffered and endured every test and temptation, so that he can help us every time we pass through the ordeals of life.

Christ Lived Our Life to Defeat Our Death

*D*id you know an early church teacher believed that Jesus was something like a spacesuit?

Apollinarius taught that God in the form of "Christ" entered into the human form of Jesus at baptism and then left him before he died, sort of like an astronaut wears a spacesuit. So according to him, "Christ" used Jesus' vocal chords to teach the disciples, for instance, but never actually became human and experienced all that humanity has to offer.

There was another early church heresy, Docetism, that challenged the idea that Jesus was a real human being, as well. Certain people inside the church, known as Gnostics, believed that Jesus only *looked* like he was a human but he really wasn't.

You see, these people couldn't wrap their minds around the idea that God, as the second person of the Trinity, would stoop so low as to become an actual human and share in all the weakness and misery of our existence.

But this is the beauty and majesty of the incarnation!

We believe God really did enter into our human experience and existence by becoming one of us. As Hebrews says, "Since all his 'children' have flesh and blood, so Jesus became human to fully identify with us" (2:14a).

I'm so glad he became "flesh and blood," just like us, because our salvation depends on our Great high priest being very human!

Why? Why do you think it's important that Jesus was an *actual* human being who actually took upon himself our flesh and blood?

Think about it: If Jesus Christ wasn't a real, live human being, how could he represent us before God? If Jesus had not been tested and tempted in every way as we are, if he had not fully experienced all that it means to be human, how could he truly offer himself as a sacrifice before God's throne?

Now this does not mean Jesus sinned or was not God. As Hebrews makes clear, Jesus is "the exact expression of God's true nature—his mirror image" (1:3), and "he was tempted in every way just as we are and conquered sin" (4:15). So Jesus is both divine and sinless.

But look at how Hebrews 2:14, 15, 18 describes what Jesus accomplished by becoming one of us:

> He did this, so that he could experience death and annihilate the effects of the intimidating accuser who holds against us the power of death. By embracing death Jesus sets free those who live their entire lives in bondage to the tormenting dread of death. … He suffered and endured every test and temptation, so that he can help us every time we pass through the ordeals of life.

Consider this: Jesus became one of us and lived our life in order to experience our death, so that he could break the power of death!

If Jesus was not really a human, he could not have been our representative before God as our utter ally. But because Jesus did truly become one of us, however, he was able to truly represent us before God as high priest and bear our solution—not only experiencing death, but defeating it in the process!

Lenten Prayer

Lord Jesus Christ, Son of God, I praise you and thank you for living life in order to experience my death—all in order to break the power of death, to rescue me and recreate me anew! Amen.

$\mathcal{D}ay\,7$

Hebrews 3:12–15

[12]So search your hearts every day, my brothers and sisters, and make sure that none of you has evil or unbelief hiding within you. For it will lead you astray, and make you unresponsive to the living God. [13]This is the time to encourage each other to never be stubborn or hardened by sin's deceitfulness. [14]For we are mingled with the Messiah, if we will continue unshaken in this confident assurance from the beginning until the end.

[15]For again, the Scriptures say,
"If only today you would listen to his voice.
Don't make him angry by hardening your hearts,
as you did in the wilderness rebellion."

Persevere By Searching Your Heart for Hiding Evil and Unbelief

Have you heard of Ryan Bell? He was the Protestant pastor who made an unusual New Year's resolution: to live for one year without God. Here's what he said on the other side of his little experiment:

"I don't think that God exists. I think that makes the most sense of the evidence that I have and my experience."

How sad!

His story and today's Lenten reading pose to us a warning:

"Search your hearts every day, my brothers and sisters, and make sure that none of you has evil or unbelief hiding within you."

Bell's story and the book of Hebrews remind us that we must stay vigilant and actively ask the Holy Spirit to do what the psalmist invited him to do:

> God, I invite your searching gaze into my heart.
> Examine me through and through;
> find out everything that may be hidden within me.
> Put me to the test and sift through all my anxious cares.
> See if there is any path of pain I'm walking on,
> and lead me back to your glorious, everlasting ways—
> the path that brings me back to you.
> (Psalm 139:23–24)

The writer of Hebrews gives us two reasons to search our hearts for evil and unbelief:

So that they won't lead us astray; so that they won't make us unresponsive to the living God.

To illustrate the powerful effect hiding evil and unbelief has on the human heart, the writer of Hebrews offers the story of his own people, the children of Israel. He says the same people whom God heard and released from Egypt refused to listen to God and rebelled. They did the very things the writer warns us of this day: "They grieved God for forty years by sinning in their unbelief…" (Hebrews 3:17).

Then what happened? They dropped dead! "God swore an oath that they would never enter into his calming place of rest all because they disobeyed him" (v. 18).

Hebrews draws our attention to an interesting aspect of our Christian life, one that is often overlooked: *perseverance*.

There is a phrase that's often abused, and it's this: "Once saved, always saved!"

While it is true we are sealed by the Holy Spirit into the family of God, not because of anything we do but because of our faith in what Christ did, time and time again the writer of Hebrews urges us to persevere in our Christian life, to remain faithful to God in both our behavior and beliefs.

Think about the story of Israel: They were God's chosen people; they were part of his family because of his grace; they experienced the blessings of that relationship. Yet Hebrews says those whose hearts were hardened—because evil and unbelief were hiding there—fell away and did not enter into God's rest.

The writer of Hebrews warns against this fate of those who were part of God's family:

"So then we must give our all and be eager to experience this faith-rest life, so that no one falls short by following the same pattern of doubt and unbelief" (Hebrews 4:11).

He goes on, and this is what we should take away in our Lenten journey:

"For we are mingled with the Messiah, if we will continue unshaken in this confident assurance from the beginning until the end."

Yes, we are united with Christ—*mingled* with the Messiah in relationship, as the writer says. But that unity requires perseverance. It requires that we hold our original conviction about Christ firmly from the beginning of our relationship until the very end.

It seems for now that Ryan Bell didn't persevere; and certainly, several children of Israel didn't, either. May we never follow their example. Instead, may we continually search our hearts for evil and unbelief.

Lenten Prayer

Holy Spirit, I invite you to search my heart for any evil or unbelief hiding within. Examine me through and through. Put me to the test, and sift me through and through. See if there is any path of pain I'm walking on. Lead me back to your glorious, everlasting ways. Amen.

$\mathcal{D}ay\ 8$

Hebrews 4:14-16

[14]So then, we must cling in faith to all we know to be true. For we have a magnificent King-Priest, Jesus Christ, the Son of God, who rose into the heavenly realm for us, and now sympathizes with us in our frailty. [15]He understands humanity, for as a Man, our magnificent King-Priest was tempted in every way just as we are, and conquered sin. [16]So now we come freely and boldly to where love is enthroned, to receive mercy's kiss and discover the grace we urgently need to strengthen us in our time of weakness.

A Power Beyond
Superhero Strength

In a recent poll of top comic book superheroes, guess who were at the top?

Perhaps it's no surprise: Superman, Batman, and Spider-Man. I would have bet on Spider-Man being the number one favorite, given how much of an everyman Peter Parker is.

Think about it: Here is a guy who is as common, ordinary, middle-of-the-road as they come. He's got job problems, family problems, and girl problems. He isn't all that strong or sensational. In fact, he's pretty weak and scrawny. It's not until an outside force acts on him when he's bitten by that radioactive spider that his weakness is transformed into strength.

It is said Spider-Man's creators wrote him with the same kind of rejection, inadequacy, and loneliness his readers could relate to. They countered this weakness by giving the costumed crusader super strength and agility, the ability to "stick" to almost any surface by shooting webbing with special "web-shooters," and giving him the power to respond to danger with a special "spider-sense." What was once weakness was transformed into strength, all because of this outside force working within Peter.

You know, many of us are like Peter Parker. We struggle with so much in life, from mundane things like leaking roofs and flat tires, to big stuff like job stress and rebellious kids. Then there is the really big stuff, like dying parents or lay-offs, and emotional baggage from teenage bullying and relational abandonment. Add to that the temptations and attacks of our enemy, and describing who we are and how we feel as "weak" doesn't do it justice!

But unlike Peter, we possess a force far more powerful than his spider bite, a power that transforms our weakness into true strength to help us overcome the many things life throws at us.

That power is the very power of Christ himself!

Our reading today from Hebrews speaks about this power, which comes at such a perfect time. Since Lent helps us contemplate our weakness and the suffering sacrifice of Christ, what better time than this to remember the incredible power and strength we all possess because Christ became weak on our behalf?

The writer of Hebrews reminds us that though we are weak and suffering from that weakness, Jesus "sympathizes with us in our frailty." The King of Kings and Lord of Lords even understands our life, *your* life, because he lived this life! But there's more, because our faith in him opens up to us access to the very throne room of God himself "to receive mercy's kiss and discover the grace we urgently need to strengthen us in our time of weakness." Though we are weak, in Christ we are strong!

This kind of power and strength is something our favorite superheroes could only dream about!

The apostle Paul experienced this power himself. In 2 Corinthians 12, Paul describes a time in his life when he was low, when he was at his weakest—all because of a so-called "thorn" in his flesh. Paul doesn't name the thorn. It could have been physical, emotional, psychological, or spiritual. The point is that while experiencing this weakness, Paul was actually strong—precisely because of what Hebrews teaches us. The strength and power of Christ was manifested and perfected in the midst of Paul's own weakness because Christ's all-sufficient grace and power rested on him.

Like Peter Parker, most of us live ordinary, average lives, often marked by rejection, inadequacy, and loneliness in various ways—and yet, Christ has strength to give us! Instead of being bitten by a radioactive spider, we've been kissed by mercy; instead of being given spider-strength, we've been given the divine strength of Christ!

Like Paul, Christ invites us to come to him and leave behind our weakness, for in him we become strong, All because Christ became weak for us on the cross.

Lenten Prayer

Jesus, sometimes I feel so weak because of the many trials of this life. Yet I am comforted knowing you understand my life and sympathize with me in my frailty. Thank you for the grace and strength to stand, which I claim this day as my own by faith! Amen.

Day 9

Hebrews 9:11-15

11But now the Anointed One has become the King-Priest of every wonderful thing that has come. For he serves in a greater, more perfect heavenly tabernacle not made by men. 12And he has entered once and forever into the Holiest Sanctuary of All, not with the blood of animal sacrifices, but the sacred blood of his own sacrifice. And he alone has made our salvation secure forever!

13Under the old covenant the blood of bulls, goats, and the ashes of a heifer were sprinkled on those who were defiled and effectively cleansed them outwardly from their ceremonial impurities. 14Yet how much more will the sacred blood of the Messiah thoroughly cleanse our consciences! For by the power of the eternal Spirit he has offered himself to God as the perfect Sacrifice that now frees us from our dead works to worship and serve the living God.

15So Jesus is the One who has enacted a new covenant with a new relationship with God so that those who accept the invitation will receive the eternal inheritance he has promised to his heirs. For he died to release us from the guilt of the violations committed under the first covenant.

What Can Wash Away Our Sins?

*I*magine that you are an Israelite living in Palestine in the year 11 AD. It is the tenth day of the seventh month in the Jewish calendar. The Day of Atonement.

You have traveled for days and ache with exhaustion, though you could care less. You are caked with sweat and dirt yet tingle with joy because you and your community are standing at the base of the glorious temple of the Lord, anticipating what is to occur deep inside its belly.

The high priest is conducting a sacred sacrificial ritual inside the temple. He has just slaughtered a young bull to atone for his and his own family's sins, a necessary step toward performing his sacred duty.

Left over are two goats. Through the casting of lots, one is selected as the animal that will perform the necessary sacrifice. The other goat will act as the so-called "scapegoat," the object upon which the sins of the community will be confessed and placed.

The high priest takes the one goat and slaughters it. He takes its blood behind the curtain into the inner sanctuary of the Tent of Meeting, sprinkling it on the various holy artifacts. He then takes more of this precious, sacrificial blood and enters into the Most Holy Place, which houses the sacred altar of the Lord. Before Yahweh himself, the high priest takes this blood and sprinkles it seven times on the horns of this altar.

After he has spread the blood of the sacrificial goat around the Most Holy Place he leaves the temple, carrying with him the second goat, the scapegoat. The crowd goes wild as the high priest descends the stairs to appear before you and the rest of Israel.

Before an awestruck crowd, the priest takes hold of the scapegoat and lays his hands upon its head. You hear him begin to confess all the sins of the people: the wickedness and unrighteousness, sins and rebellion; the list is long and agonizing.

After this confession he takes the goat and gives it to a caretaker, who then takes it away from you and the people outside the city, releasing it into the wilderness. This scapegoat symbolically and literally carries upon itself your sins and the sins of all Israel.

Back at the temple before the people the high priest lifts his hands and shouts with great confidence, "It has been done! Sacrifice has been made for the sins of the people!" In response you and your people erupt in song and dance and shouts of joy. You cry out in praise to the Lord your God for providing atonement for sins for yet another year.

Now, what is so interesting about this scenario is that there will always be *another* tenth day of the seventh month—another Day of Atonement. Year after year after year this high priest had to continually offer sacrifices for the sins of the people, because, you see, these sacrifices could not ultimately *take away* those sins.

That is until around 33 AD when our Great high priest, Jesus Christ, entered into the real Most Holy Place once and for all.

By his own blood.

This is how Hebrews describes the work of Jesus Christ in our above reading!

He is both the sacrificial lamb and the scapegoat; he shed his blood and took upon himself our guilt—all to cleanse our consciences, making us white as snow!

You see, no amount of religious ritual or human effort could ultimately remove our guilty stain. God had to take it upon himself to do that.

This Lenten season, let Hebrews 9 and this old hymn reminds us of this:

What can wash away my sin?
Nothing but the blood of Jesus;
What can make me whole again?
Nothing but the blood of Jesus.
Oh! precious is the flow
That makes me white as snow;
No other fount I know,
Nothing but the blood of Jesus.[*]

---

[*] Robert Lowry, "Nothing But the Blood," Public Domain, pub. 1876.

Lenten Prayer

Jesus, I recognize that it is only your blood that can wash away my sins, rescue me from death, wash me clean, and make me whole again. I thank you and praise your holy name for shedding that blood for me! Amen.

Day 10

Hebrews 10:11–18

¹⁰By God's will we have been purified and made holy once and for all through the sacrifice of the body of Jesus, the Messiah!

¹¹Yet every day priests still serve, ritually offering the same sacrifices again and again—sacrifices that can never take away sin's guilt. ¹²But when this Priest had offered the one supreme sacrifice for sins for all time, he sat down on a throne at the right hand of God, ¹³waiting until all his whispering enemies are subdued and turn into his footstool. ¹⁴And by his one perfect sacrifice he made us perfectly holy and complete for all time!

¹⁵The Holy Spirit confirms this to us by this Scripture, for the Lord says,

¹⁶"Afterwards, I will give them this covenant:
I will embed my laws into their hearts
and fasten my Word to their thoughts."
¹⁷And then he says,
"I will not ever again
remember their sins and lawless deeds!"
¹⁸So if our sins have been forgiven and forgotten, why would we ever need to offer another sacrifice for sin?

Christ's Once-for-All Sacrifice

*D*o you ever get this nagging feeling like there's something else left for you to do to become right with God?

Maybe it's after you've messed up by sinning against God or your neighbor.

You lied to your boss about why that report isn't yet finished, or maybe you had a lustful thought toward your coworker. Then you feel like you need to double-down on the religious rituals you think will earn God's favor once more. You vow to read an extra passage of Scripture or go to Sunday morning *and* evening services for the next two months!

All to offer some sort of sacrifice for those sins.

If you haven't read our passage today, go and read it now.

Boy, do I love this imagery! It is so rich and pregnant with meaning. And the message it carries is fabulous news for you and me: No more sacrifice is needed!

The author begins by comparing what Jesus did on the cross to what the ancient priests of Israel did in the temple. As the author describes, every day the priests of Aaron stood serving and sacrificing in the temple—they never sat down; they remained standing because their sacrifices had to be repeated day after day, year after year!

None of the sacrifices of the old way could remove sin, permanently cleanse our heart, or provide the heart transplant we so desperately needed.

Not so with Jesus; with him it's totally different!

While the old high priests remained standing, what did Jesus do?

He sat down! Why?

Because he declared on the very blood-soaked beams of execution that held his limp, lifeless body that it was finished!

It's over with; no more sacrifice is needed!

For those of us who are in Christ, we are no longer blamed for ruining creation with our sin. We are no longer guilty for rebelling against God because of Jesus Christ.

Because God the Father sacrificed his one and only Son, we are no longer guilty!

Because of Jesus we have eternal forgiveness. We have been cleaned. We have a new heart. Because of Jesus' sacrifice, God has "made us perfectly holy and complete for all time!" (Hebrews 10:14).

Friend, that's *you*!

Because your Great high priest sacrificed himself for your sins, your rebellious acts are no longer remembered by the very Creator whom you have rebelled against.

And because of the loving, gentle, caring Jesus no more sacrifice is needed!

Do you believe that this day? Do you believe that it is finished?

Or do you have this lingering desire for some way to somehow atone for your own sins? To somehow earn God's favor or work for salvation?

Drink deep this reality: We do not need to strive to earn God's favor. We do not need to perform to make God love us more than he already did through the cross. We do not need to work for salvation to appease God.

Our Great high priest became one of us so that he could fully identify with us and understand our brokenness and weakness—all so that he could provide the final sacrifice that would *finally* cleanse us from our sin and *finally* make us new!

May we remember deep down this Lenten season that Jesus truly paid it all. And all to him we owe!

Lenten Prayer

Jesus, thank you for remembering my sins no more and doing everything necessary, once and for all, to forgive me and make me whole again! Amen.

Day 11

Psalm 65:1–5

[1-2]O God in Zion, to you even silence is praise!
   You are the God who answers prayer;
   all of humanity comes before you with their requests.
[3]Though we are overcome by our many sins,
   your sacrifice covers over them all.
[4]And your priestly lovers, those you've chosen,
   will be greatly favored to be brought close to you.
   What inexpressible joys are theirs!
   What feasts of mercy fill them in your
      heavenly sanctuary!
   How satisfied we will be just to be near you!
[5]You answer our prayers with amazing wonders
   and with awe-inspiring displays of power.
   You are the righteous God who helps us like a Father.
   Everyone everywhere looks to you,
   for you are the Confidence of all the earth,
   even to the farthest islands of the sea.

Help Is Already Here!

There's this story about a hurricane that came to a coastal town. An emergency warning went out letting people know the waters were going to rise and flood nearby homes. Everyone was told to evacuate immediately.

One man, however, heard the warning, but decided to stay, praying, "God, if I am in danger I know you will send a miracle to rescue me! So I will stay put and trust you."

That afternoon as the man stood on his porch watching the water rise, a man in a canoe came by and called to him, "Neighbor, get in!" But the man again refused. "No, I trust God will save me."

By evening the man had to seek safety on the second floor. A rescue boat came by and saw him in the window. "Sir, climb out of the window and into our boat!" they shouted. But the man refused again. "Save someone else, because I trust God will rescue me!"

By nightfall the man had to climb onto his roof because the flood was so high. Later a helicopter was flying overhead and spotted him with its searchlight. They lowered a ladder and told the man to grab ahold of it so they could pull him up. Still he refused. "No thanks! I believe God will save me!"

After midnight, the floodwaters swept the man away and he drowned. When he reached heaven, the man stood before

God and questioned him: "God, I believed you would save me, so I prayed to be rescued! Why didn't you?"

And God said, "Yes, I heard your prayers! That's why I sent you a warning, a canoe, a rescue boat, and a helicopter."

The moral of the story? God has already done everything necessary to save and rescue us. Help is *already* here!

Like our friend caught in the torrential rainfall, we were all in big trouble. As the psalmist said: We were "overcome by our many sins." Sometimes we can forget God has done everything necessary to rescue us from drowning in them! God is the God who answers prayer, because his "sacrifice covers over them all."

Some of us might be looking for something else to save and rescue us: hoping the good we do outweighs the bad; performing religious rituals to make us clean; looking to some other method to relieve us of our guilt.

We're all like the man watching the flood of our sins rise and rise, praying and trusting God to do something about it. And yet, God the Father's response is like the one in our story: "Friend, I've heard your prayers for rescue, that's why I sent you my Son, Jesus!"

The psalmist declares God answers our prayers "with amazing wonders, and with awe-inspiring displays of power." The first wonder and powerful display was when God became one of us through virgin birth, and was named Jesus. And then for three years Jesus displayed his wonders and power through a ministry of mighty miracles. Finally, the most wondrous, powerful display was through his sacrificial death to cover our sins and his triumphal resurrection—defeating sin, shame, guilt, and death in the process!

This Lent, be like the man in our story, but go one step further: Trust God fully to rescue you, but then wholly lean on the One he already sent to save you—his Son.

Lenten Prayer

Father, I thank you and praise you for already doing everything necessary to rescue me from the rising tide of my sin and its consequences: death. This day I renew my trust in the finished work of your Son, who lives and reigns with you and the Holy Spirit, now and forever. Amen.

Day 12

Romans 1:16–20

[16]I refuse to be ashamed of sharing the joyful message of God's liberating power unleashed in us through Christ! For I am thrilled to preach that everyone who believes is set free—the Jew first, and to people everywhere! [17]This gospel unveils within us a continual revelation of God's righteousness—a perfect righteousness given to us when we believe! And it moves us from receiving life through faith, to the power of living by faith! This is what the Scripture means when it says,

"We are right with God through life-giving faith!"

[18]For God in heaven unveils his holy anger breaking forth against every form of sin, both toward ungodliness that lives in hearts and evil actions. For the wickedness of humanity deliberately smothers the truth and keeps people from acknowledging the truth about God. [19]In reality, the truth of God is known instinctively, for God has embedded this knowledge inside every human heart. [20]Opposition to truth cannot be excused on the basis of ignorance, because from the creation of the world, the invisible qualities of God's nature have been made visible, such as his eternal power and transcendence. He has made his wonderful attributes easily perceived, for seeing the visible makes us understand the invisible! So then, this leaves everyone without excuse.

The Good News to God's Wrath

"*D*o you want the good news or the bad news first?" You've probably heard this setup to a number of well-worn jokes. Did you know there was a recent scientific study that showed the answer to this question depends on whether you are giving or receiving the bad news?

A researcher at the University of California showed if you are the one receiving the news, an overwhelming majority of people wanted the bad news first. Apparently, if people know they're going to get bad news, they just want to get it over with, and ending with good news ends on a high note. But if you're the bearer of bad news, you're usually anxious about giving it, and want to hold off on sharing it first—who wants to give bad news, anyway?

The researcher's advice is that it's better to give the bad news first, and then the positive news to help people accept their bad news.

But there's an alternative method, too. It's what the researcher calls "the sandwich approach." It goes like this: "Your lab results came back and your cholesterol is down. By the way, your blood pressure is seriously high. But your blood sugar levels are super good!" You see how the doctor "sandwiched" the bad news in between two pieces of good news?

Perhaps this was the strategy Paul used to explain our own bad news, good news situation.

You see, every single person on the planet has a problem: we're in big trouble, because we're rebels deserving of God's wrath.

Here's how Paul describes this problem: God's "holy anger" is coming against "every form of sin, both toward ungodliness that lives in hearts and evil actions"; our wickedness "deliberately smothers the truth" about God; everyone is "without excuse" because God has made himself known to the world; we've "refused to honor him as God or even be thankful for his kindness"; we've "entertained corrupt and foolish thoughts about what God was like"; our hearts are "misguided...steeped in moral darkness"; we are "shallow fools"; we worship and serve "the things God made rather than the God who made all things"; God has given us over to our "disgraceful and vile passions"; and because of this we "deserve to die" (Romans 1:18–32).

Yikes! If this isn't the very definition of bad news, I don't know what is!

And yet—pay attention, here—there is no need to fret! Because despite this very bad news, there is even better, more amazing news:

"We are right with God through life-giving faith!"

The gospel is the very definition of *good* news; it's the good news to God's wrath.

Before he gets to our super bad news, Paul gives us a glimpse of the super amazing news to come: there is a "liberating power unleashed in us through Christ"; everyone who believes in Christ "is set free"; the good news of Jesus "unveils within us a continual revelation of God's righteousness"; and this right standing with God is "given to us when we believe."

In the week to come, Paul dives deeper into this good news. Because of Jesus' love story: we have been powerfully acquitted of our rebellion (3:24); we are "liberated…from the guilt, punishment, and power of sin" (3:24); perfect righteousness is credited to our account "when we believe and embrace the one who brought our Lord Jesus back to life" (4:23); "we can enjoy true and lasting peace with God" (5:1); God declares, "You are now righteous in my sight!" (5:9); "we are at peace with God" (5:10); and our former identity as a rebellious sinner "is forever deprived of its power!" (6:6).

So, yes, we had a problem, so Paul gives us some pretty bad news. But before and afterwards is the most amazing news we could ever receive!

I love how Paul answers our age-old question! Like the researcher suggests, he sandwiches the bad news of God's wrath between the good news of the gospel: Because of Christ's gospel we are declared righteous before God's throne—all because of his extravagant grace, mercy, and love!

Lenten Prayer

Jesus, as I consider the bad news of my story I am comforted by the good news of yours. This day I stand in the power of your gospel, knowing that through it I am loved, forgiven, liberated, and at peace! Amen.

$\mathcal{D}ay\ 13$

Romans 3:21–26

[21-22]But now, independently of the Law, the righteousness of God is tangible and brought to light through Jesus, the Anointed One! This is the righteousness that the Scriptures prophesied would come! It is God's righteousness made visible through the faithfulness of Jesus Christ. And now all who believe in him receive that gift! For there is really no difference between us, [23]for we all have sinned and are deprived of God's divine splendor. [24]Yet through his powerful declaration of acquittal, God freely gives away his righteousness! His gift of love and favor now cascades over us, all because Jesus the Anointed One has liberated us from the guilt, punishment, and power of sin!

[25]Jesus' God-given destiny was to be the sacrifice to take away sins and now he is our Mercy Seat because of his death on the cross. We come to him for mercy for God has made a provision for us to be forgiven by faith in the sacred blood of Jesus. This is the perfect demonstration of God's justice, because until now, he had been so patient—holding back his justice because he heard the echo of his likeness in human hearts. So he covered over the sins of those who lived prior to Jesus' sacrifice. [26]And when the season of tolerance came to

an end, there was only one possible way for God to give away his righteousness and still be true to both his justice and his mercy—to offer up his own Son. So now, because we stand on faith in Jesus, God declares us righteous in his eyes!

Not Responsible and Not Guilty

There's this story about a guy who was pulled over for going fifty-five in a thirty-five. As you can imagine, he got a nice three-by-seven-inch piece of paper for doing so! He didn't want the points so he went to traffic court. Lucky for him, the police officer didn't show. So he got out of paying for his nice shiny piece of paper.

What's interesting about this story is what the judge said to the offender. Because the police office didn't show, the judge declared him "not *responsible*." Not responsible.

It wasn't that he wasn't guilty—that couldn't be determined because the police office didn't show up. So he was declared not responsible.

Friend, if you've trusted God's promised gift of rescue by believing that Jesus' death paid your price and his resurrection from the dead gives you new life—you get both verdicts!

First, you are "not responsible." In our reading Paul makes clear at one point that's all we were—everyone was responsible for being a rebel because "we all have sinned and are deprived of God's divine splendor." We should have been the ones to pay the price for our sins—in fact Paul says that death is our "meager wages" for those sins (Romans 6:23).

But Jesus took upon himself that responsibility. *He* was the one who was led to the slaughterhouse and beaten for your sins against God. *He* was the one who crawled up on that altar of wooden beams and then bled out all over the soil beneath them. *He* was the faithful one, when we were utterly faithless.

Jesus, the Son of God, took responsibility for every one of our sins so that we wouldn't have to. And because he did— God offers us the gift, the *promise* of a "not guilty" verdict on the day of judgment. He actually *makes* us not guilty for all of our sins, because of the sacred blood of Jesus.

As Paul says in our reading, "through his powerful declaration of acquittal, God freely gives away his righteousness! His gift of love and favor now cascades over us, all because Jesus the Anointed One has liberated us from the guilt, punishment, and power of sin!"

Because of Christ, God has acquitted us of the charges against us. He has liberated us from the punishment and power of sin, stamping a big "not guilty!" verdict on our rap sheet!

This isn't something we can earn—Paul makes it clear this verdict is independent from any sort of religious ritual or former religious law. It comes to us *purely* by way of the love of

God through his Son. Now all that's required is to believe, to trust his promised gift by faith.

It's funny, because Paul calls this "the perfect demonstration of God's justice." Doesn't that seem odd? It seems like if God were to perfectly demonstrate his justice, he'd hold *us* responsible, he'd declare *us* "guilty!" for our rebellion against him!

Yet he does the exact opposite. He's the one who takes responsibility for our sins, doing everything necessary by offering up his Son as payment. It was the only way he could stay true to his own justice and mercy.

Now where does that leave us? "[B]ecause we stand on faith in Jesus, God declares us righteous in his eyes!"

Lenten Prayer

Lord Jesus Christ, Son of God, I am humbled that you chose to take responsibility for my sins by dying for them, and I thank you for the power and truth of my "not guilty" verdict! Amen.

Day 14

Romans 4:18–25

[18]Against all odds, when it looked hopeless, Abraham believed the promise and expected God to fulfill it! He took God at his word and as a result he became the father of many nations. God's declaration over him came to pass:

"Your descendants will be so many
that they will be impossible to count!"

[19]In spite of being nearly one hundred years old when the promise of having a son was made, his faith was so strong that it could not be undermined by the fact that he and Sarah were incapable of conceiving a child. [20-21]He never stopped believing God's promise, for his faith transferred God's power to him to father a child. And because he was mighty in faith and convinced that God had all the power needed to fulfill his promises, Abraham glorified God!

[22]So now you can see why Abraham's faith was "credited to his account as righteousness before God." [23]And this declaration was not just spoken over Abraham, [24]but also over us. For when we believe and embrace the one who brought our Lord Jesus back to life, perfect righteousness will be credited to our account as well. [25]Jesus was handed over to be

crucified for the forgiveness of our sins and was raised back to life to prove that he made us right with God!

Credited to Our Account as Righteousness

*W*hat is faith? What does it mean to "have faith" or "put your faith" in someone or something? How does that *look* to have faith?

It seems like such a pie-in-the-sky idea, having faith. Paul gives us the perfect story to make it clear what it means and what's required of us—the story of Abraham.

Perhaps you know that story well from the book of Genesis. As the story goes at the beginning of chapter 12, one day God visits Abraham and gives him a promise:

I will make a great nation out of you. I will bless you. I will make your name great. People who curse you will be cursed. But people who bless you will be blessed. In fact all nations will be blessed through you Abraham and your children. So go from your land, your family, your father's household to the land I will show you.

That's Abraham's promise. But in order to get it he had to leave behind his former way of life and trust God—he had to believe God "in faith" by following him forward into this new future.

Imagine how hard this must have been for Abraham. At the time he was around seventy-five. He had property and a safe, secure household. He had everything he could ever need or want. And God wanted him to leave all of it behind?

Yet that's exactly what Abraham did! He got up and followed God into his promised future on faith, trusting that God would fulfill his promise to not only give him the land but also give him the family.

And this faith and trust in God's word—his promise to save and provide—is what forms this relationship between Abraham and God. Abraham's faith in God's promise saves him. In Genesis 15 we read that Abraham believed and God credited that belief—that faith and trust—to him as righteousness.

Back to our reading. I love what Paul says of Abraham, here:

In spite of being nearly one hundred years old when the promise of having a son was made, his faith was so strong that it could not be undermined by the fact that he and Sarah were incapable of conceiving a child. He never stopped believing God's promise, for his faith transferred God's power to him to father a child.

Amazing! Literally, the original language says that Abraham knew his body was "as good as dead" and that Sarah's womb was "dead"—meaning they were very old! Even though his situation seemed hopeless, Abraham trusted God; he believed what God said. He had faith in God and his power to make good on his promise.

And Paul compares *our* hopeless situation to Abraham's and his trust in God's promise to provide to our own trust in God's promise of rescue through Christ alone. Such trust in the finished work of Christ on the cross as payment for our own Promised Land and spiritual family "credits righteousness" into our spiritual account, so to speak.

Remember what the writer of Hebrews said about faith? "Now faith brings our hopes into reality and becomes the foundation needed to acquire the things we long for. It is all the evidence required to prove what is still unseen" (Hebrews 11:1).

Jesus was put to death for our rebellion and was raised to new life so that our debt to God could be marked "paid in full!" We get that status—"not guilty," "paid in full"—by trusting in God's promised gift by believing that Jesus' death and resurrection can do for me what I can't do for myself.

That's what it means to have faith.

May we have the hope of Abraham, continuing to trust in the sufficiency of the suffering sacrifice of Christ, knowing "he was handed over to be crucified for the forgiveness of our sins and was raised back to life to prove that he made us right with God!"

Lenten Prayer

God, this day I hope with Abraham, knowing that by trusting your promise of new life through the death and resurrection of Christ, you have credited to my account your righteousness—making me right with you forever! Amen.

Day 15

Romans 5:1-2, 6-10

[1]Our faith in Jesus transfers God's righteousness to us and he now declares us flawless in his eyes! This means we can now enjoy true and lasting peace with God, all because of what our Lord Jesus, the Anointed One, has done for us! [2]Our faith guarantees us access into this marvelous kindness which has given us a perfect relationship with God. What incredible joy bursts forth within us as we celebrate our hope of sharing God's glory!

[6]For when the time was right, the Anointed One came and died to demonstrate his love for sinners who were entirely helpless, weak, and powerless to save themselves.

[7]Now who of us would dare to die for the sake of a wicked person? And we can all understand if someone was willing to die for a truly noble person, [8]yet who has ever heard of someone dying for an evil enemy? But Christ proved God's passionate love for us by dying in our place while we were still lost and ungodly!

[9]And there is still much more to say of his unfailing love for us! For through the blood of Jesus we have heard the powerful declaration—"You are now righteous in my sight!" And because of the sacrifice of Jesus, you will never experience

the wrath of God! [10]So if while we were still enemies, God fully reconciled us to himself through the death of his Son, then something greater than friendship is ours. Now that we are at peace with God and because we share his resurrection life we are brought to perfection!

Who Ever Heard of Such a Thing!

We've all heard those heroic stories or seen those heroic movies where someone laid down their life for a friend, comrade, or loved one. Or did their professional or civic duty by putting themselves in harm's way for a stranger.

The soldier lays on a grenade to save his platoon. The firefighter climbs back into the burning house for a child and tosses him or her out of the third story to rescuers below, only to be overtaken by the roaring flames inside. The husband pushes his wife out of the way of an oncoming bus, taking upon himself its impact.

Any one of us might perform the same heroic acts for the people we love or for truly good people who would otherwise be harmed.

How about for a wicked person? I mean a truly evil and bad man or woman? Would you lay down your life for Osama bin Laden, Saddam Hussein, or Kim Jong-il? Or how about someone less extreme, like your adulterous coworker who's destroyed families or the neighborhood gossip who's destroyed reputations? How about those people?

You might not want to admit it, but at one point each of us was in their same boat. And we were totally helpless, weak, and powerless to do anything about it; we could not save ourselves!

Amazingly, at just the right moment when everything was lost and hopeless, the King of Kings and Lord of Lords stepped into our story to rescue us from ourselves and our eternal destination—

By dying for us!

Think about that: Jesus died for the dictator as much as the adulterer; he died for the gossip as much as the warlord; he died for the terrorist as much as he died for you and me!

This is remarkable, I know. Paul thought so, too. He wondered, "Who of us would dare to die for the sake of a wicked person?" Good question! Who of us would die for bin Laden or that coworker? I can't imagine any of us. For a "truly noble person," as Paul says, maybe. But "who has ever heard of someone dying for an evil enemy?" Paul asks.

The point is *no one!* No one would have taken the bullet in place of bin Laden; none of us would have volunteered to be hanged so that Hussein didn't have to die that way.

And yet…get this: "Christ proved God's passionate love for us by dying in our place while we were still lost and ungodly!"

Who ever heard of such a thing!

If that isn't love, I mean true, sacrificial, unfailing, *passionate* love—then I don't know what is!

What's even more amazing, is that this passionate, unfailing love of our Father didn't stop with Christ's sacrifice. Not only did Jesus die for us; he gave us all the blessings and advantages of his life, too. Through Christ's blood, we are righteous in God's eyes. We will never experience God's wrath; our relationship with our creator was repaired. We are not only friends with God—we are at peace with him; and because we have been raised to new life with Christ, we are in the process of being fully put back together again!

Bin Laden was America's enemy. At one point we were God's enemy, too. Yet instead of shedding our blood like the US did bin Laden's, God shed his own blood for us. May we never grow weary of remembering the lengths to which God went to express his passionate, unfailing love by laying down his life for us!

Lenten Prayer

Lord Jesus Christ, Son of God, thank you for the cross! Thank you for shedding your blood for my soul while I was still a sinner, an enemy of God, in order to give me the blessings of divine sonship. Amen.

Day 16

Romans 6:1–2, 5–7, 11–14

[1]So what do we do then? Do we persist in sin so that God's kindness and grace will increase? [2]What a terrible thought! We have passed away from sin once and for all as a dead man passes away from this life. So how could we live under sin's rule a moment longer?

[5]For if we are permanently grafted into him to experience a death like his, then we are permanently grafted into him to experience a resurrection like his and the new life that it imparts.

[6]Could it be any clearer that our former identity is forever deprived of its power? For we were co-crucified with him to dismantle the stronghold of sin within us, so that we would not continue to live one moment longer submitted to sin's power.

[7]Obviously, a dead person is incapable of sinning.

[12]Sin is a dethroned monarch and must no longer continue its rule over your life; controlling how you live and compelling you to obey its desires and cravings! [13]So then, refuse to answer its call to surrender your body as a tool for wickedness. Instead passionately answer God's call to present your body to him, for you were once dead, but now you've experienced

resurrection life! You live now for his pleasure, ready to be used for his noble purpose. [14]Remember this: sin will not conquer you, for God already has! You are not governed by law but governed by the reign of the grace of God!

No Longer Be Slaves to Sin

*O*ne of the greatest scourges on the history of Western nations is that of forced human slavery. Think about it: Europeans and Americans bought and traded other humans, simply because they were from another continent and had a different skin color.

A classic work on the evil and immorality of slavery in America is *Uncle Tom's Cabin*. Harriet Beecher Stowe's fictional tale weaves together accounts of the realities of slavery. Consider this passage from her book:

> He was possessed of a handsome person and pleasing manners, and was a general favorite in the factory. Nevertheless, as *this young man was in the eye of the law not a man, but a thing, all these superior qualifications were subject to the control of a vulgar, narrow-minded, tyrannical master.* This same gentleman, having heard of the fame of George's invention, took a ride over to

the factory, to see what this intelligent chattel had been about. He was received with great enthusiasm by the employer, *who congratulated him on possessing so valuable a slave* (emphasis added).[*]

The rest of the book describes the kind of life slaves have as possessions under "vulgar, narrow-minded, tyrannical" masters.

Now imagine escaping such a life of tyranny through the Underground Railroad to the North, say to Ohio or Illinois. Having found freedom, who in their right mind would return back to the "death" experience of slavery? Who would return to the bondage and humiliation, the decay and torture? Who would trade in their free identity for their former enslaved one?

Obviously these are rhetorical questions designed to make a point—the same one Paul is making in our Lenten reading for today.

Like those former Southern slaves, we have escaped from death to life, from slavery to freedom, from one identity to an entirely new one. Why, then, would we return to our former way of life by persisting in sin?

If Christ has freed us from the power of sin and death, "How could we live under sin's rule a moment longer?"

Good question! Paul goes on to expound upon the nature

---

[*] Harriet Beecher Stowe, *Uncle Tom's Cabin* (New York: Barnes and Noble Classics, 2003), 13.

of our new identity apart from the slavery of sin: we have been "permanently grafted into [Christ] to experience a resurrection like his and the new life that it imparts"; "our former identity is forever deprived of its power"; "the stronghold of sin within us" has been "dismantled"; and, here's the kicker, "sin is a dethroned monarch!"

While the blood of countless Civil War soldiers emancipated slaves throughout the Union from the conditions of earthly slavery, the blood of Jesus has emancipated you and me from the conditions of spiritual slavery! Because of this earthly battle, Southern slaves were no longer governed by the Southern slave laws. Now, because of Christ's epic battle on the cross, Paul says "You are not governed by law but governed by the reign of the grace of God!"

Western slavery was ugly and brutal, transforming Africans into mere "things," possessed by others like a horse or pair of trousers. If you can imagine it, our slavery to sin was even more ugly and more brutal—transforming us from statues of God into the walking dead, zombies transfixed by sin's siren call of wickedness.

But now, because of the precious blood of Christ, because we have died with him and been raised to new resurrection life—we who have been adopted into God's family as joint heirs to the promises of Christ are free! Free from the power of sin and death, free from suffocating guilt and shame, and free to live as God intended us to live when he created us.

Now, live not as a slave, but as the free person you are!

Lenten Prayer

Heavenly Father, I thank you and praise your holy name for freeing me from the power and bondage of sin through the death and resurrection of your Son. Help me to live as I really am: your free child who is governed by the reign of your grace! Amen.

Day 17

Psalm 32:1–6, 8–10

[1]How happy and fulfilled are those
　　whose rebellion has been forgiven,
　　those whose sins are covered by blood!
[2]How blessed and relieved are those
　　who have confessed their corruption to God!
　　For he wipes their slates clean
　　and removes hypocrisy from their hearts.
[3]Before I confessed my sins, I kept it all inside;
　　my dishonesty devastated my inner life,
　　causing my life to be filled with frustration,
　　irrepressible anguish, and misery.
[4]The pain never let up, for your hand of conviction
　　was heavy on my heart.
　　My strength was sapped, my inner life dried up
　　like a spiritual drought within my soul.

Pause in his presence

[5]Then I finally admitted to you all my sins,
　　refusing to hide them any longer.
　　So I said, "My life-giving God,
　　I'll openly acknowledge my evil actions."

And you forgave me!
All at once the guilt of my sin washed away
and all my pain disappeared!

Pause in his presence

⁶This is what I've learned through it all:
Every believer should confess their sins to God;
do it every time God has uncovered you
in the time of exposing.
For if you do this, when sudden storms of life overwhelm,
you'll be kept safe.
⁸⁻⁹I hear the Lord saying, "I will stay close to you,
instructing and guiding you along the pathway
for your life.
I will advise you along the way
and lead you forth with my eyes as your guide.
So don't make it difficult, don't be stubborn
when I take you where you've not been before.
Don't make me tug you and pull you along.
Just come with me!"
¹⁰So my conclusion is this:
Many are the sorrows and frustrations
of those who don't come clean with God.
But when you trust in the Lord for forgiveness,
his wrap-around love will surround you.

Does God Have to Tug and Pull You Along?

"*Y*ou can lead a horse to water, but you can't make it drink," the Old English proverb goes.

The picture, here, is one of a strong, stubborn four-legged creature being led by bridle and bit to a brook of bliss to quench its thirst. The only thing the horse's master can do is lead it to the source of water, tugging and pulling it if he must. Once there, however, he can't make it drink; the horse has to do the rest.

Translation: Like horses, people will only do what they've made up their mind to do.

Sometimes we can be like that, can't we? We know what we're supposed to do when asked to keep the confidence of a friend, but later we gossip about them behind their back. Or when our boss asks us why that report still isn't finished, we tell a "white lie" to cover our tracks. Sometimes the sin is even worse. The Holy Spirit may try to lead us into truthful ways, but our heart yanks back on the reigns and insists on a different way because we've already made up our mind—leading to pain and misery.

King David describes this phenomenon perfectly in today's reading:

I hear the Lord saying, "I will stay close to you,
instructing and guiding you along the pathway
    for your life.
I will advise you along the way
and lead you forth with my eyes as your guide.
So don't make it difficult, don't be stubborn
when I take you where you've not been before.
Don't make me tug you and pull you along.
Just come with me!"

What a humorous picture: God tugging with all his might
on the "bit and bridle" of our heart—saying through gritted
teeth, "Would you just come with me already!"

Realize that this isn't anger; it's exhaustion from trying to
guide and train us out of his deep, deep love for us. The Lord
has in mind for us nothing but our best. Like any good father,
he will do everything to help us along this path—only better!
This is exactly what Proverbs 3:11–12 teaches:

My child, when the Lord God speaks to you,
never take his words lightly,
and never be upset when he corrects you.
For the Father's discipline comes only
from his passionate love and pleasure for you.
Even when it seems like his correction is harsh,
it's still better than any father on earth gives to his child.

After quoting this very passage, the writer of Hebrews encourages us to "fully embrace God's correction as part of your training, for he is doing what any loving father does for his children." He goes on to say, "We all should welcome God's discipline as the validation of authentic sonship. For if we have never once endured his correction it only proves we are strangers and not sons" (12:8). God trains and corrects out of his deep Father-love!

We need this poem this seventeenth day of Lent, not only because it reminds us not to be like the horse when it comes to God's leading and correction, but because it is a poem of thanksgiving. The psalmist isn't lamenting, here; he is thanking God for his heavy hand, for sapping his strength, for drying up his inner spirit.

Why? Because afterwards he finally admitted his sins! And when he did, "All at once the guilt of my sin washed away, and all my pain disappeared!" Once David finally gave into God's yanking on the bridle of his heart, he experienced blessing and relief, forgiveness and cleansing.

We experience all of what David experienced, too, when we repent and confess our sins, allowing God to lead us to his brook of bliss *and* drink deeply of his forgiveness.

And when you do, "His wrap-around love will surround you!"

Lenten Prayer

Lord, I thank you for your correction, guidance, and discipline, knowing that it validates my sonship and is the only way to blessing and relief! Amen.

Day 18

Ephesians 1:3–10

³Everything heaven contains has already been lavished upon us as a love gift from our wonderful heavenly Father, the Father of our Lord Jesus—all because he sees us wrapped into Christ. This is why we celebrate him with all our hearts!

⁴And he chose us to be his very own, joining us to himself even before he laid the foundation of the universe! Because of his great love, he ordained us as one with Christ from the beginning, so that we would be seen as holy in his eyes with an unstained innocence.

⁵For it was always in his perfect plan to adopt us as his delightful children, ⁶so that his tremendous grace that cascades over us would bring him glory—for the same love he has for his Beloved One, Jesus, he has for us!

⁷Since we are now joined to Christ, we have been given the treasures of salvation by his blood—the total cancellation of our sins—all because of the cascading riches of his grace. ⁸This superabundant grace is already powerfully working in us and flooding into every part of our being, releasing within us all forms of wisdom and practical understanding. ⁹And through the revelation of the Anointed One, he unveiled his

secret desires to us—the hidden mystery of his long-range plan, which he was delighted to implement from the very beginning of time. [10]And this detailed plan will reign supreme through every period of time until the fulfillment of all the ages finally reaches its climax—when God makes all things new in all of heaven and earth through Jesus Christ.

The Blessing of Spiritual Adoption

*I*f you've ever known an adopted child and an adopting family, you know how very special adoption is. Perhaps you know first hand the uniqueness of adoption, because you yourself were adopted or you've adopted a boy or girl into your family.

The reason why adoption is so special is because it transforms a tragic situation into one of bounty and blessing for a little boy or girl longing for a mama and papa to call their own.

I can't imagine an adoptive family treating that child less than the full member of the family they really are, can you? Adoptive parents are as thrilled to embrace their new child as a full son or daughter as they are to be embraced as parents. And they give them all the rights and privileges as if they were genetically born into their family.

How silly—and wrong—it would be if the adoptive child had to sit in a different room at a different table during dinner. Imagine if they were left behind during the yearly family summer vacation. If adoptive parents take their role seriously, they will treat their adoptive daughter or son as if they were their genetic own.

Do you know that if you're a Christian, *you've* been adopted? That's right. You've been spiritually adopted into God's family! Your tragic situation has been transformed into triumph because of that adoption. You've been given all the rights and privileges of God's family, too.

I love the language Paul uses to describe who we really are as full, complete children of God:

> For it was always in his perfect plan to adopt us as his delightful children, so that his tremendous grace that cascades over us would bring him glory—for the same love he has for his Beloved One, Jesus, he has for us!

Yes, you read that right: God, the creator and sustainer of every molecule in the universe, has adopted you as his delightful child! Not only that, but the same love the Father has for his Beloved Son, Jesus, is the kind of love he has for you!

Just as an adopted son or daughter has access to all the treasures of their household—love and praise, vacations and holidays, food and entertainment—so too have the treasure storehouses of heaven been opened up to us! Look at some of what Paul says we have since we've been joined to Christ and adopted into God's family: our sins have been totally cancelled; God's superabundant grace is at work in our lives; and all forms of wisdom and practical understanding are released within us.

Like earthly adoption, our heavenly adoption took a tragic situation and transformed it into a triumphant one, for you and me. If you ever doubted the love God has for you—even for one second—meditate on this heavenly reality, the same one the apostle John wrote about in his first letter:

> Just look at the magnificent, over-flowing love the Father has generously heaped on us, that he would consider us his adoptive children—brothers and sisters, that's who we really are! (1 John 3:1)

May we know this heavenly reality deep down as we continue journeying toward the object that paved the way for our adoption in the first place: the cross of Christ.

Lenten Prayer

Heavenly Father, what love you have lavished on me, that I should be called your child! Thank you for always planning to adopt me; thank you for loving me the same way you love your own Son! Amen.

Day 19

Ephesians 2:1–7

¹And his fullness fills you, even though you were once like corpses, dead in your sins and offenses. ²It wasn't that long ago that you lived in the religion, customs, and values of this world, obeying the dark ruler of the earthly realm who fills the atmosphere with his authority, and works diligently in the hearts of those who are disobedient to the truth of God. ³The corruption that was in us from birth was expressed through the deeds and desires of our self-life. We lived by whatever our natural cravings and thoughts our minds dictated, living as rebellious children subject to God's wrath like everyone else.

⁴But God still loved us with such great love. He is so rich in compassion and mercy. ⁵Even when we were dead and doomed in our many sins, he united us into the very life of Christ and saved us by his wonderful grace! ⁶He raised us up with Christ the exalted One, and we ascended with him into the glorious perfection and authority of the heavenly realm, for we are now joined as one with Christ!

⁷Throughout the coming ages we will be the visible display of the infinite, limitless riches of his grace and kindness, which was showered upon us in Jesus Christ.

The Dead Now Live Because of God's Great Love

*I*f you were around in the 1980s then the name Jeffrey Dahmer probably sounds familiar to you. Jeffrey was known as the Milwaukee Cannibal—a serial killer who killed seventeen men and boys between 1978 and 1991.

What you may not know is that Jeffrey became a Christian. During a news interview, Jeffrey said this about his faith:

I've since come to believe that the Lord Jesus Christ is the true creator of the heavens and the earth, it didn't just happen. And I have accepted him as my Lord and Savior, and I believe I, as well as everyone else, will be accountable to him.[*]

On November 28, 1994, Jeffrey was beaten to death by another inmate. Yet if the above testimony is true, that means right now he is in heaven with Christ and will one day be judged in him and be raised to new life.

How do you feel about that? That a serial killer will escape eternal judgment and enjoy the new heavens and the new earth, right along with all of us for all eternity?

Some of the strongest reaction to the news that Jeffrey had trusted God's gift of grace in Christ came from Christians. Pastor Roy Ratcliff baptized Jeffrey after he had put his faith in

---

[*] Stone Philips, "Confessions of a Serial Killer: Jeffrey Dahmer Speaks," *Dateline*, February 1994.

Jesus. A common question he got from Christians was about the sincerity of Jeffrey's faith. He said, "My answer is always the same: Yes, I am convinced he was sincere. This question bothers me. Why question the sincerity of another person's faith?"

He goes on: "Jeff was judged not by his faith, but by his crimes. The questioner always seemed to hope I'd answer, 'No, he wasn't sincere.' The questioner seemed to be looking for a way to reject Jeff as a brother in Christ instead of seeing him as a sinner who has come to God. The subtext of such questions was simple. They didn't want to think of Jeff as a brother. Such ungraciousness is contrary to the Christian spirit."*

Pastor Roy is absolutely right! God's grace is as big as the world and as deep as our darkest sins—which is a good thing. Because at one point all of us we were just like Jeffrey.

Maybe you didn't commit the same kinds of evil acts as he did, but the Bible makes it clear that all of us were in the same kind of trouble: "You were once like corpses, dead in your sins and offenses"; we "lived in the religion, customs, and values of this world," so that we obeyed the Dark Ruler; we were corrupted "from birth"; before Christ we lived any which way we wanted, to the point we were considered "rebellious children subject to God's wrath like everyone else."

That's quite the indictment—one that's not too far off from Jeffrey's!

Despite all of this—despite all of these evil acts and sinful

* Beliefnet, "Saving Jeffrey Dahmer," November 2006, www.belief net.com/Faiths/Christianity/2006/11/Saving-Jeffrey-Dahmer.aspx.

offenses, despite living as rebels, "God still loved us with such great love!"

Throughout the Bible we read about this God—a God who is gracious and compassionate, a God who is slow to anger and abounding in love. Our God relents from sending calamity and destruction—from the Israelites to the Ninevites, from Jeffrey to you and me and everyone else!

What Paul says is remarkable: Even though each of us were "dead and doomed" because of our many and various sins, God "united us into the very life of Christ and saved us by his wonderful grace!" Not only that, "we are now joined as one with Christ," having been raised to brand new life and been given "the glorious perfection and authority of the heavenly realm!"

In other words, the dead now live—all because of God's great love! And now we are statues of that love. We are visible displays of the "infinite, limitless riches of his grace and kindness, which was showered upon us in Jesus Christ."

Even people like Jeffrey. Even people like you and me.

Lenten Prayer

Oh great God, I thank you for your great love! At one point I was dead and doomed, by now I am saved and alive—all because of your grace and kindness, which you showered on me in Jesus Christ. Amen.

Day 20

Ephesians 4:22–32

22And he has taught you to let go of the lifestyle of the ancient man, the old self-life, which was corrupted by sinful and deceitful desires that spring from delusions. 23Now it's time to be made new by every revelation that's been given to you. 24And you will be transformed as you embrace the glorious Christ-within as your new life and live in union with him! For God has re-created you all over again in his perfect righteousness, and you now belong to him in the realm of true holiness. 25So discard every form of dishonesty and lying so that you will be known as one who always speaks the truth, for we all belong to one another in one body.

26So be passionate! But don't let the passion of your emotions lead you to sin! Don't let anger control you or be fuel for revenge, not for even a day. 27Don't give the slanderous accuser, the devil, an opportunity to manipulate you! 28If any one of you has stolen from someone else, never do it again. Instead, be industrious, earning an honest living, and then you'll have enough to bless those in need.

29And guard your speech—never let ugly or hateful words come from your mouth, but instead let your words become beautiful gifts that encourage others; do this by speaking words of grace to help them.

³⁰The Holy Spirit of God has sealed you in Jesus Christ until you experience your full salvation. So never grieve the Spirit of God or take for granted his holy influence in your life. ³¹Lay aside bitter words, temper tantrums, revenge, profanity, and insults. ³²But instead be kind and affectionate toward one another. Has God graciously forgiven you? Then graciously forgive one another in the depths of Christ's love.

Out with the Old, In with the New!

*S*pringtime is the perfect time to clean the house and get rid of the clutter. It just feels right. Perhaps that's why there are so many neighborhood sales come late spring through early summer!

During these months garages and yards are filled with the old to make way for the new: Old TVs sit at the end of driveways to make room for the latest models bought over the holidays; old clothes hang from ladders and sit atop card tables to provide space in drawers and closets for new ones; baby toys are sold to make room for toddler toys, and toddler ones make way for teen ones.

As the saying goes: "Out with the old, in with the new!"

There are times when we need to do a little "spring clean-ing" in our lives, too. And, actually, the Lenten season is the perfect time to consider how we can get rid of even more of our old-self behaviors to become more like our new self we have become through Christ.

Now, understand that this is an ongoing process. Yet this process is one Paul calls us to actively engage in, just as much as we do each year with our homes. Throughout our reading selection today, Paul gives us several important instructions:

He tells us to "let go" of the manner of living we used to live in our old self-life; to "discard" lying and dishonesty; to not let our passionate emotions lead us into sinning; to con-trol our anger; to prevent the devil from manipulating us; to no longer steal; to be careful what we say, never letting hate-ful words come from our mouths; to never grieve the Spirit of God and take for granted how he has impacted our lives; and finally, to drop any and all "bitter words, temper tan-trums, revenge, profanity, and insults."

That's quite the list! In the same way we trade our old stuff for new stuff, Paul exhorts us to exchange our old self-life for our new life in Christ:

He tells us to "be made new" and live in complete union with him; to tell the truth to one another; to earn an honest living and bless those in need; to breathe words as "beauti-ful gifts" that are encouraging and gracious; to "be kind and affectionate toward one another"; and to lovingly forgive each other out of the depths of Christ's own love he has for us.

The reason why we consider the way we're living and do a little "house cleaning" in our life isn't to make God love us more; it isn't to religiously perform to earn his approval—we've already got that love; he already approves of us! No, the reason why is because he died for us and forgave us, and now we do for others what God has done for us!

Having received God's love and forgiveness, we now carry the experience of what his love is like and have become vessels to carry his love and forgiveness to others. How else could we respond than to let go of the lifestyle from our former life and jump in, with both feet, into the new life of Christ—giving everything we've got in utter devotion to the one who gave it all to save us, all for God's glory.

Lenten Prayer

Holy Spirit, thank you for sealing me in Jesus Christ until I experience salvation to its fullest! May I never grieve you or take for granted your holy influence in my life. May you empower me to discard the old self-life and fully live the Christ-within life in greater measure. Amen.

Day 21

Ephesians 5:8–17

⁸Once your life was full of sin's darkness, but now you have the very light of our Lord shining through you because of your union with him. Your mission is to live as children flooded with his revelation-light! ⁹And the supernatural fruits of his light will be seen in you—goodness, righteousness, and truth. ¹⁰In this revelation-light, you will learn to choose what is beautiful to our Lord.

¹¹And don't even associate with the servants of darkness because they have no fruit in them; instead, reveal truth to them. ¹²The very things they do in secret are too vile and filthy to even mention. ¹³Whatever the revelation-light exposes, it will also correct, and everything that reveals truth is light to the soul. ¹⁴This is why the Scripture says, "Arise, you sleeper! Rise up from the dead and the Anointed One will shine his light into you!"

¹⁵⁻¹⁶Don't live foolishly as those with no understanding, but live honorably with true wisdom, for we are living in evil times. Take full advantage of every day as you spend your life for his purposes. ¹⁷And then you will have discernment to fully understand God's will.

Who Are You?
A Child of Revelation-Light!

Here's to the crazy ones. The misfits. The rebels. The troublemakers. The round pegs in the square holes. The ones who see things differently. They're not fond of rules. And they have no respect for the status quo. You can quote them, disagree with them, glorify or vilify them. About the only thing you can't do is ignore them. Because they change things. They push the human race forward. And while some may see them as the crazy ones, we see genius. Because the people who are crazy enough to think they can change the world, are the ones who do.[*]

*I*f you're an Apple fan, you had visions of iMacs and iPhones dancing in your head. Because at "Here's to the crazy ones" your mind went back in time to their ingenious Think Different ad campaign.

Do you remember this memorable campaign from the late 1990s? Within months of returning to Apple in 1996,

---

[*] CBS News, "Steve Jobs thought different," Oct. 5, 2011, describing the ad campaign created with Chiat/Day, which debuted September 28, 1997, www.cbsnews.com/news/steve-jobs-thought-different.

Steve Jobs helped launch this marketing effort to reintroduce Apple to the masses after the catastrophic reign of Gil Amelio.

The commercials were this montage of artists and actors, inventors and influencers ranging from Amelia Earhart to Albert Einstein, Jim Henson to John Lennon and Yoko Ono. And of course, Jerry Seinfeld.

While the commercials were designed to reintroduce Apple to the world, they actually served a much more important purpose.

The *real* reason? To help Apple remember who they were.

In his biography, Steve was quoted as saying, "We at Apple had forgotten who we were. One way to remember who you are is to remember who your heroes are. That was the genesis of that campaign."

At the beginning of Apple's new season of astronomical growth and prosperity, Steve wrote the above script that brought his people back to the basics of what it meant to be the people of Apple.

Sometimes we Christians need the same thing. We need to be reminded of who we are and what we are called to do—how we are called to live as children of Christ's revelation-light. That's Paul's purpose in our reading for today. He reminds us that at one point our life was full of sin's darkness. *Now*, however, we have the very light of our Lord shining in and through us because we have been united with him.

What that means is that we are to live in such a way that God's revelation-light floods us, overflowing with the supernatural fruits of goodness, righteousness, and truth. He encourages us to "live honorably with true wisdom," rather than "foolishly as those with no understanding," to "take full advantage of every day as you spend your life for his purposes," so that we will be able to fully discern and understand God's will.

On the flipside, it also means that we aren't even to associate with the servants of darkness anymore, because of the kind of fruit they produce—"The very things they do in secret are too vile and filthy to even mention," Paul says. Instead, he instructs us to reveal truth to them, because "whatever the revelation-light exposes, it will also correct, and everything that reveals truth is light to the soul."

Nearly twenty years ago, Apple's Think Different campaign helped remind their community who they were and what they were called to do. I love how their ad ends: "Because the people who are crazy enough to think they can change the world, are the ones who do." Steve's rallying cry for his employees was to dream and create "insanely great" computer products for the masses, and change the world along the way.

Paul gives a similar rallying cry for us this day as much as his:

"Arise, you sleeper! Rise up from the dead and the Anointed One will shine his light into you!"

Lenten Prayer

Lord, I want nothing more than to faithfully shine as your child of light. Help me to live honorably with true wisdom, rather than foolishly as those with no understanding. I ask for your help this day to take full advantage of every day, so I can spend my life living for your purposes and your purposes alone! Amen.

Day 22

Ephesians 6:10–18

[10]Now finally, my beloved ones, be supernaturally infused with strength through your life-union with the Lord Jesus. Stand victorious with the force of his explosive power flowing in and through you.

[11]Put on the full suit of armor that God wears when he goes into battle, so that you will be protected as you fight against the evil strategies of the accuser! [12]Your hand-to-hand combat is not with human beings, but with the highest principalities and authorities operating in rebellion under the heavenly realms. For they are a powerful class of demon-gods and evil spirits that hold this dark world in bondage. [13]Because of this, you must wear all the armor that God provides so you're protected as you confront the slanderer, for you are destined for all things and will rise victorious.

[14]Put on truth as a belt to strengthen you to stand in triumph. Put on holiness as the protective armor that covers your heart. [15]Stand on your feet alert, then you'll always be ready to share the blessings of peace as you subdue your enemies.

[16]In every battle, take faith as your wrap-around shield, for it is able to extinguish the blazing arrows coming at you from the evil one! [17-18]Embrace the power of salvation's full

deliverance, like a helmet to protect your thoughts from lies. And take the mighty Spirit-sword of the spoken Word of God.

Arm Yourself!

*I*t's remarkable how the modern soldier has been transformed over the past several hundred years.

During the Revolutionary War, one of the reasons the colonists were so successful is because the English "Red Coats" insisted on fighting the old-fashioned way in, well, bright red coats—a dead giveaway in the New World! Fast forward to World War I and part of the reason the deaths were so high on all sides was because the Europeans employed tactics and equipment from the eighteenth century to fight a twentieth-century war—sort of like bringing spitballs to a bowling ball fight!

Since then militaries around the world have wizened to what it takes to keep soldiers equipped and protected, as best as possible. Consider some of the standard equipment issued to the US infantry: a personal weapon, either an M4 or M9, with appropriate sights and grips; layered sleep system, consisting of a sleeping bag, liners, and bivy sack; personal hydration system; helmet; personal first aid kit; night vision headgear; their uniform; communication devices; and a personal locator beacon.

That's a lot of equipment—a lot of vital equipment that's necessary to help American soldiers complete their task and stay alive.

Now, if the modern soldier wouldn't think about stepping foot on enemy soil or walking into a battle without this standard-issue equipment, why would any of us who have been called by Christ into as dangerous of a mission forsake our own equipment?

Thankfully, we have our own standard-issue equipment straight from heaven's arsenal. In fact, the equipment we've been issued is the same full suit of armor that God wears when he goes into battle! Here's the list of equipment: the belt of truth; a holy "heart covering"; feet coverings of readiness; a wrap-around shield of faith; the helmet of salvation; and last, but certainly not least, the mighty Spirit-sword.

What's interesting about this list is that it's almost a mirror image of the standard issue equipment given to Roman soldiers during the day Paul was writing to encourage Christian "soldiers":

Just as soldiers prepared for vigorous activity with a leather apron or "belt" to secure their clothing, we do the same with the truth of God's Word; a piece of armor covered their chest to protect them from bows and arrows, where holiness protects our "heart" from the accusatory arrows of Satan; Roman soldiers wore half-boots to prepare them for long marches, and we do the same through the long Christian journey when we stand in Christ's peace; Roman shields were long and wide to protect the soldier's entire person, which faith does for the believer; solid bronze helmets covered and protected soldiers from devastating blows to the head, and the knowledge we are rescued from sin and death and raised to new life performs the same task for believers' minds; and finally, the Spirit-sword of the spoken Word of God is like the Roman short sword used in close combat and defensively, which defends us and fights for us with penetrating power.

As with any good soldier, we must properly prepare for battle each day by taking advantage of our standard-issue equipment, which is God's very own armor! The goal of wearing it is to take our stand in the onslaught of accusations, temptations, tricks, and schemes of our enemy.

Yet, though we have a powerful enemy who plots and strategizes to take us out, though our Christian journey is one of struggle, thanks be to Christ we already stand in victory with the full, explosive power of God flowing in and through us!

Lenten Prayer

God, this day I take my stand against every plot and scheme the enemy might plan against me by wearing your full armor, believing that with it I am victorious with the force of your explosive power flowing in and through me! Amen.

Day 23

Psalm 1

[1]What delight comes to those who follow God's ways!
    They won't walk in step with the wicked,
    nor share the sinner's way,
    nor sits in the circle of scoffers.
[2]Their pleasure and passion is remaining true
      to the Word of "I Am,"
    meditating day and night in his true revelation of light.
[3]They will be standing firm like a flourishing tree
    planted by God's design,
    deeply rooted by the brooks of bliss;
    bearing fruit in every season of their lives.
    They are never dry, never fainting,
    ever blessed, ever prosperous.
[4]But how different are the wicked.
    All they are is dust in the wind—
    driven away to destruction!
[5]The wicked will not endure the day of judgment,
    for God will not defend them.
    Nothing they do will succeed or endure for long,
    for they have no part with those who walk in truth.

⁶But how different it is for the lovers of God!
> The Lord watches over them as they move forward
> while the paths of the godless lead only to doom.

What You Sow You Shall Reap

A common nineteenth-century saying offers some sound words of wisdom for the start of our fourth full week of Lent:

> We sow a thought and reap an act;
> We sow an act and reap a habit;
> We sow a habit and reap a character;
> We sow a character and reap a destiny.
> What truth, what wisdom!

Notice the progression, here, from a simple thought to an entire life trajectory. That's how most things go, don't they?

The person who needs to lose a few pounds didn't get there overnight. It started with the desire to eat one more cookie before bed. And then they did. Before long that desire has transformed into an extra-cookie-eating habit, leading to those extra pounds.

I'm reminded of the 1980s antidrug campaign that said "Nobody says, 'I wanna be a junkie when I grow up.'" Of course not! It starts with a thought of escaping through one joint or hit, which leads to the act itself. Before long becoming a junkie is indeed that person's destiny.

In many ways Reade echoes Psalm 1. In this ancient Hebrew poem, the psalmist warns of what comes when a person joins the wicked and then *becomes* wicked.

Notice the progression: He goes from simply "walking in step" with sinners to sharing in their way. It's like the kid who merely hangs around and walks with neighborhood troublemakers. He doesn't do what they're doing—breaking windows or egging cars and the like.

Not yet, anyway. Because eventually he'll join in; they usually do. He'll "share the sinner's way." Before long he'll "be found sitting in the scorner's seat." Not only will he break the windows and egg the cars—he'll have a seat at the table, directing the troublemaking from the throne of power!

Not so for the lovers of God. Instead, they desire to follow God's ways! Instead of walking in wicked ways, they meditate on God's ways; instead of sharing in sin, they're standing in God's "revelation light"; instead of sitting at the seat of the sinners' table and eating the fruit of evil, they're bearing God-pleasing fruit "in every season of their lives!" Their pleasure for God leads to meditation on his Word, which leads to standing in it and bearing good fruit from it.

It is true that thoughts lead to actions, actions lead to habits, habits lead to a character, and a character leads to a destiny.

What is the destiny of the wicked and the lovers of God?

The psalmist declares that the wicked, sinners, and scorners "will not endure the day of judgment." They will be "driven away to destruction"; their path leads "only to doom."

But for lovers of God who follow God's way, it's totally different! Instead their destiny is one of flourishing: "They are never dry, never fainting; Ever blessed, ever plentiful."

Let's get honest now that we're just over halfway through our Lenten journey:

What are the thoughts, actions, habits, and character you're sowing? Are they tilling a path that leads to the destiny of the godless? Or are they paving the way for a destiny of the flourishing that God promises his lovers?

Ask God to shape them for the sake of reaping a destiny of delight!

Lenten Prayer

Heavenly Father, I want nothing more than for my thoughts, actions, habits, and character to be shaped by you and you alone! May you give them deep roots in your brook of bliss, so that I may reap a wholly Christ-shaped destiny.

Day 24

Matthew 7:21-27

[21]"Not everyone who says to me, 'Lord, Lord,' will enter into the realm of heaven's kingdom. It is only those who persist in doing the will of my heavenly Father! [22]On the day of judgment many will say to me, "Lord, Lord, don't you remember us! Didn't we prophesy in your name? Didn't we cast out demons and do many miracles for the sake of your name? [23]But I'll have to say to them, 'Go away from me, you lawless rebels! I've never been joined to you!'

[24]"Everyone who hears my teaching and applies it to their lives can be compared to a wise man who built his house on an unshakable foundation. [25]For when the rains fell and the flood came, with fierce winds beating upon his house, it stood firm because of its strong foundation.

[26]"But everyone who hears my teaching and does not apply it to their lives can be compared to a foolish man who built his house on sand. [27]For when it rained and rained and the flood came, with wind and waves beating upon his house—it collapsed and was swept away!"

Which Person Are You:
Wise or Foolish?

*E*ach of us long to build a good life, a life that lasts. Isn't that why we make resolutions every New Year?

We resolve to lose weight, get organized, or quit smoking. We vow to spend less and save more, stay fit and healthy, or spend more time with family. All in an effort to build the good life.

Jesus has a word about what it takes to build a life that lasts.

At the end of his famous Sermon on the Mount, Jesus tells a fascinating story about two kinds of people: wise people and foolish people.

Jesus says the wise person builds his house on the rock—a solid foundation. The *other* person, however—the foolish person—builds his house on sand.

Jesus is doing what a lot of ancient teachers did: He is setting up two possibilities and using sharp contrasts to grab our attention and force us to think about how we are living, where we are going, and who we are following—and then make a choice.

Throughout the Bible the act of building and the idea of foundations are common metaphors for *learning* and *living*. Jeremiah speaks of a king building his palace on unrighteousness and injustice. Paul speaks of Jesus as the cornerstone to our foundation.

So there are *good* foundations and there are *bad* foundations. Or to use Jesus' words: *wise* foundations and *foolish* foundations. And these foundations lead to good and bad living.

Most of us would agree that building a shack upon sand dunes along a lakeshore would be pretty foolish. Why? Because inevitably rains will come down, the streams will rise, and wind will blow and beat against the house—whether on a foundation of rock or a foundation of sand.

Throughout the Hebrew Scriptures storm language is used both of life's difficulties and of God's judgment. What's fascinating in Jesus' story is that both the wise builder and foolish builder experience the same storm—the same difficulties and judgment.

Building a house on solid rock doesn't protect you *from* troubles, it protects you *in* them. The same is true of God's judgment at the end of our story.

Part of what Jesus is talking about is a person's entire life in the presence of God's final judgment. And every one of us, wise builder or foolish builder, will have to give an account of that life—a life lived either in Christ, or not.

We're all building a house on some sort of foundation. Jesus says that we are either building wisely or foolishly.

But then he goes one step further: He makes the claim that we are building wisely only when we hear *his* words and then do them.

In essence what Jesus is saying is that our security in this life and the next depends entirely upon our response to *him*. And anyone who hears Jesus' words and does not do them is a fool.

What if he's right?

What if *his* moral and ethical vision for how we are to live our lives is the right way? What if it's the *wise* way? The *only* wise way?

What if he's right that everyone who hears his words of his *and* obeys them is wise? But everyone who hears his words and *doesn't* obey them is foolish?

What if Jesus is right that *his* way is the way into the life that we were meant to live—the kind of life that all of us thirst for?

If he is, that if you follow his teachings and obey him you are wise and will build a life that lasts—if he's right then the obvious question is:

Are you following and obeying him?

Lenten Prayer

Lord, I realize that your way is the only way to live and the only way you've called me to live. Help me be a wise person by listening to your words and then living them as the foundation of my life. Amen.

Day 25

Matthew 11:28-30

[28]"So everyone, come to me! Are you weary, carrying a heavy burden? Then come to me. I will refresh your life for I am your oasis. [29]Simply join your life with mine. Learn my ways and you'll discover that I'm gentle, humble, easy to please. You will find refreshment and rest in me. [30]For all that I require of you will be pleasant and easy to bear."

Come to Me...
and I Will Give You Rest!

Over the past few weeks since starting our journey toward the cross, you have been invited to take stock of how you are following Christ.

During the first full week you were invited to "search your hearts...and make sure that none of you has evil or unbelief hiding within you" (Hebrews 3:12).

At the beginning of the week you were asked: "What are

the thoughts, actions, habits, and character that you're sowing? Are they tilling a path that leads to the destiny of the godless? Or are they paving the way for a destiny of flourishing as a God promises his lovers?"

And then yesterday: Are you following and obeying Christ?

While it may be uncomfortable to engage in such self-evaluation, at times it is crucial for our ongoing life with Christ. Lent provides the perfect opportunity to consider how we are walking our journey as Christians in response to the suffering and sacrifice of Jesus.

But here's the thing: You're not alone in your journey!

Because the very person whom you are called to follow is your oasis! He promises he is "gentle, humble, easy to please." In him you will find "refreshment and rest."

He is the very opposite of a sage on a stage; instead, he's a guide on the side!

Unlike other spiritual teachers who have handed down laws and religious rituals, not only does Jesus claim he is gentle, humble, and easy to please, he says he is there with you along the way—at your side, guiding and helping you.

Jesus' invitation to "join your life" with his carries with it the image of farm animals being joined together with what was called a "yoke."

Back in the day, a wooden crosspiece was fastened over the necks of two or more animals and attached to a plow or cart. Together they would drag the plow over the hard soil, loosening it so the farmer could plant his seed. Or they would pull a cart full of logs, boulders, or the year's harvest.

As you can imagine, for one ox or horse to do that kind of work would have been grueling. But for two or four, tied together with this wooden yoke, it was far more manageable.

Jesus is inviting you to do the same with your life! To join it to his in order to live what he teaches. Along the way he promises to refresh you and give you rest.

God makes the same promise through his servant Paul. After urging the Philippians, "Continue to allow your new life to manifest through you as you live in the holy awe of God," he makes this promise:

"God will continually revitalize you, implanting within you the passion to accomplish the good things you desire to do" (Philippians 2:12–13).

Some of us are carrying heavy burdens of past sin. Maybe you're carrying them on your own, trying to escape the shame and guilt the enemy binds you with.

Let Jesus take away that burden and give you rest from your past!

Some of us are carrying heavy burdens of present temptation and struggle. We want nothing more than to live the kind of life God calls us into and obey him—yet it's such a struggle; it's so wearying trying to live that life, like a single ox plowing a field.

Let Jesus take away that burden, give you rest, and revitalize you for the journey ahead of following and obeying him!

You see, that's the hope of Lent. On the other side of this journey stands a cross, where God not only declares us not guilty and erases our criminal record because of Christ—he helps us live on the other side of prison!

In light of this do what hymnist George Bennard did: Cherish and cling to the old rugged cross, knowing that at its foot is refreshment and rest in the one who hung there.

Lenten Prayer

Jesus, thank you for the promise that you are gentle, humble, and easy to please as I seek to follow and obey you. Thank you for suffering and dying for me, in order to pardon and sanctify me! This day I come to you, bringing my heavy burdens of sin and temptation, seeking refreshment and rest. Amen.

Day 26

Matthew 13:3–9

"Consider this: There was a farmer who went out to sow seed. [4]As he cast his seed, some fell along the beaten path and the birds came and ate it. [5]Other seed fell onto gravel that had no topsoil. The seeds quickly shot up, [6]but when the days grew hot the sprouts were scorched and withered, because they had insufficient roots. [7]Other seeds fell among the thorns and weeds, so when the seeds sprouted, so did the weeds, crowding out the good plants. [8]But other seeds fell on good rich soil that kept producing a good harvest. Some yielded thirty, some sixty, and some even one hundred times as much as he planted! [9]If you're able to understand this—then you need to respond!"

If You're Able to Understand—Respond!

*I*n marketing there is this tactic known as a "call to action." Wikipedia defines it as "an instruction to the audience to provoke an immediate response." It goes something like this:

At the end of an e-mail advertisement, say for your favorite clothing store, there will usually be a graphic that implores you to do something. Maybe the sale is a twenty-four-hour sale, so you need to "act fast!" or "buy today!" The e-mail could be introducing a new line of jeans, so they want you to "find out more." Or "visit a store today" beckons you to the nearest shop to "claim your free gift!"

Companies believe that without this direct call, consumers won't know what to do next. Or rather, won't do what they *want* you to do next, and that's take action—preferably by swiping your credit card to make a purchase!

The same could be said of Jesus' own message about God's kingdom realm.

Along with his glorious message of rescue and new life comes a big bright flashing "call to action" that invites—no, *requires*—people to respond, to do something with what he says.

To help get this point across to his disciples, he told a story meant to illustrate spiritual truths. We call it a *parable*. He told lots of these simple stories. And this one focuses our attention on the responsibility of listening to, understanding, and then responding to Jesus' message.

After describing four soils that represent four kinds of people, he explained his spiritual story in this way:

He said, "The seeds that fell on the beaten path represent the heart of the one who hears the message of the kingdom realm but doesn't understand it. The adversary then comes and snatches away what was sown into his heart" (Matthew 13:19).

Those grown on gravel "represent the person who gladly hears the kingdom message, but his experience remains shallow" (v. 20). After he hears the message, "troubles and persecutions come," but he quickly leaves it behind, "for the truth didn't sink deeply into his heart" (v. 21).

The third person represents those who have received Jesus' message, but it is suffocated by "all of life's busy distractions, his divided heart and ambition for wealth"; they prevent him "from bearing spiritual fruit" (v. 22).

Finally, the seed that fell in rich, good soil represents people "who hear and fully embrace the message of the kingdom realm of heaven," resulting in their lives bearing good fruit—so much so that the harvest is "thirty, sixty, even one hundred times as much as was sown" (v. 23).

Now, here's the question: Which soil are you?

The way Jesus ended his little story makes it clear that a willingness to hear and obey is necessary for our relationship with God.

In other words, we need to respond to Jesus' call to action!

God's gracious message and invitation "seed" to join and experience all that his kingdom realm has to offer—forgiveness of our rebellion, rescue from sin and death, release from shame and guilt, new life—is scattered to all people. That's what's constant and stable. The variable, however, is the response of the "soils" that seed is spread to.

Jesus warns against superficial hearing and an open heart that quickly changes to a hard heart based on shifting circumstances. He warns against allowing other things to get in the way of hearing, as well.

For Jesus, a listening heart is a receptive heart! So how do you know if the soil of your heart is listening, obedient, and receptive? Think about it: How do you know if a tree or bush is healthy and planted in good soil?

By its fruit!

So, perhaps another question we should ask is: How's your fruit?

Like any tree, the presence (or lack thereof) is a good indication of the health of the soil. Take time, then, to invite the Spirit of God to reveal how it is you are hearing, understanding, and receiving the Son's declaration of the Father's invitation to God's kingdom realm.

Lenten Prayer

Spirit of God, which soil am I? Have I listened to your message and received it like good soil? Or have I allowed the enemy, the cares of this world, and the distractions of life snatch it away? Search my heart and reveal to me my fruit, so that I may delight in your message and walk in your ways. Amen.

Day 27

Matthew 15:11–20

¹¹What truly contaminates a person is not what they put into their mouths but what comes out of their mouths! That's what makes them defiled."

¹²Then his disciples approached him and said, "Don't you know that what you just said offended the 'separated ones?'"

¹³Jesus replied, "Every plant that my heavenly Father didn't plant is destined to be uprooted. ¹⁴Stay away from them, for they're nothing more than blind guides. Do you know what happens when a blind man pretends to guide another blind man? They both stumble into a ditch!"

¹⁵But Peter spoke up and said, "Will you explain to us what you mean by your parable."

¹⁶Jesus said, "Even after all that I've taught you, you still remain clueless? ¹⁷Is it hard to understand that whatever you eat enters the stomach only to pass out into the sewer? ¹⁸But what comes out of your mouth reveals the core of your heart. Words can pollute, not food. ¹⁹You will find living within an impure heart evil ideas, murderous thoughts, adultery, sexual immorality, theft, lies, and slander. ²⁰That's what pollutes a person, eating with unwashed hands doesn't defile anyone."

What's Your Problem?

*A*re we sinners because we sin, or do we sin because we're sinners?

Perhaps you've heard this question before. It's one Christians have been asking for generations. It's important to get the answer to this question right, because it impacts the solution to our problem. There's no better time to consider it than during this season of contemplating and celebrating the suffering and sacrifice of Christ.

Jesus touched on this question, actually, in one of his run-ins with the so-called "separated ones," the Jewish religious teachers of his day. They wondered why the disciples didn't ceremonially wash their hands before they ate, accusing them of ignoring the ancient religious traditions of the elders and suggesting they were defiled because of it.

Jesus responds with a sort of parable, illustrating that our problem isn't in external things and acts—it's at the heart level.

He taught, "Whatever you eat enters the stomach only to pass out into the sewer." In other words, your standing before God isn't affected by what you eat that ends up in the toilet! On the flip side, your *right* standing before God isn't affected by external religious rituals, either—like ceremonial hand washing or going to church three times a week.

You see, our problem isn't merely that we've failed to live

up to a set of external moral and religious standards. Our problem is way deeper than that.

Our problem isn't an external one; it's an internal one.

Jesus makes this clear when he said, "What comes out of your mouth reveals the core of your heart." Which means we needed a whole *new* heart in order to become right with God!

This is why we could do nothing on our own to solve our problem. How could we? If the things we do on the outside don't make us impure, as Jesus says, then how could we think religious acts like ritual hand washing could purify us?

Because, you see, in answer to our question, we sin because we're sinners—not the other way around.

People do impure things, because we *are* impure. Before Christ, we lie because we're liars, we gossip because we're gossipers, and we hate because we are haters.

Our problem needed a God-sized—no, *cross-sized*— solution! It took an act of God, literally, to wash us and make us pure. Jesus paid the price, in our place, for all the wickedness within us in order to forgive us, cleanse us, and make us new.

So, friend, how's your heart? I ask, because that should be our true focus, not only during our Lenten journey, but throughout our Christian journey, too.

Jesus is saying to pay careful attention to our heart; we can't ignore the true source of our problem—the inner reality of the heart. Thankfully, because of what Jesus did, he offers us a brand-new heart that is set free from the compulsion to sin.

We could say that on the cross Jesus was the ultimate heart surgeon. He suffered those beatings and accusations; he broke open his body and shed his blood.

All to give you a new heart—a pure, cleansed, undefiled heart!

Lenten Prayer

Lord Jesus Christ, Son of God, have mercy on me! Thank you for paying the ultimate price, in my place—all so that I can be purified and cleansed of my sins and given a new, undefiled heart! Amen.

Day 28

Matthew 16:21–27

²¹From then on Jesus began to clearly reveal to his disciples that he was destined to go to Jerusalem and suffer injustice from the elders, leading priests, and religious scholars. He also explained that he would be killed and three days later be raised to life again.

²²Then Peter took him aside to correct him privately. He reprimanded Jesus over and over saying to him, "God forbid, Master! Spare yourself. You must never let this happen to you!"

²³Jesus turned to Peter and said, "Get out of my way, you Satan! You are an offense to me, because your thoughts are only filled with man's viewpoints and not with the ways of God!"

²⁴Then Jesus said to his disciples, "If you truly want to follow me, you should at once completely reject and disown your own life. And you must be willing to share my cross and experience it as your own, as you continually surrender to my ways. ²⁵For if you choose self-sacrifice and lose your lives for my glory, you will continually discover true life. But if you choose to keep your lives for yourselves, you will forfeit what you try to keep. ²⁶For even if you were to gain all the wealth and power of this world with everything it could offer you—at the cost of your

own life, what good would that be? And what could be more valuable to you than your own soul? ²⁷It has been decreed that I, the Son of Man, will one day return with my messengers, and in the splendor and majesty of my Father. And then I will reward each person according to what they have done.

Will You Share Christ's Cross?

*I*n 2014, the radical Muslim group Boko Haram killed or abducted nearly four thousand people—mostly Christians. Later that year ISIS, the Muslim group from Syria, forced tens of thousands of Christian men, women, and children to flee for their lives under the threat of similar persecution. Religious leaders warned it was fast becoming a genocide.

Similar stories of suffering and sacrifice have been told for generations—from modern China and the Soviet Union to the Muslim conquests of the Middle Ages and further back to Roman persecution of the early church.

Yet, isn't this what Jesus predicted would happen?

Before his death, Jesus told his disciples, "Just remember, when the unbelieving world hates you, they first hated me. … Because you won't align yourself with the values of this world, they will hate you" (John 15:18–19).

We hear these stories and can't comprehend what it's like to fear for our life and suffer—all for claiming the name of

Christ. And yet, Jesus not only warned this would happen but taught that we must be willing to share in this experience—because Christ himself suffered and died.

He predicted this would happen even before it did, which made one disciple hopping mad! After Jesus revealed he would suffer and be killed at the hands of the Jewish religious leaders, Peter took him aside and basically chewed him out:

"God forbid, Master! Spare yourself. You must never let this happen to you!"

How did Jesus respond? "Get out of my way, you Satan!"

(I wouldn't recommend following Jesus' example and using this as a comeback!)

"You are an offense to me," Jesus continues, "because your thoughts are only filled with man's viewpoints and not with the ways of God!"

What's the deal? Why this reaction?

You see, in those days the Jewish people were expecting a warrior-king who would come riding in to fight Israel's final fight, drive their Roman oppressors from the land, and renew the nation. This was most likely Peter's expectation, too. And he knew what others knew: A dead messiah was a failed messiah! Others had come before Jesus claiming to be the Anointed One, only to find themselves crucified by Rome as terrorists.

So when Jesus predicted and claimed the same fate, it makes sense why Peter would react so strongly. Yet not only did Peter not have a clue about who Jesus was and what Jesus was called to do—it seems Peter wasn't at all interested in that mission!

Hence Jesus' strong rebuke and the following sermon on what it truly means to follow Jesus and be his disciple.

True discipleship means "a willingness to reject and disown your own life"; following Jesus means a willingness "to share in [Christ's] cross and experience it as your own"; it requires choosing "self-sacrifice and [losing] your lives for [Jesus'] glory."

In other words, if you would claim the name of Christ and follow him with your life, you must be willing to lose that life and suffer for his name—just like Jesus did.

Interestingly, Peter did follow Jesus' footsteps, literally! Church history tells us that Peter shared the same fate of Jesus; he was crucified, but upside down, at his insistence.

Would you be willing to travel the same road of suffering, shame, and death as Peter, and the scores of other martyrs from the first century all the way to the present?

Maybe suffering doesn't look the same way for you as it does for Nigerians or Iraqis—but losing a promotion, friends, and family because you're a Christian can be hard, too.

Consider the number of ways Christ might be calling you too lose your life and share his cross—all for his glory!

Lenten Prayer

Jesus, help me to lose my life and be willing to suffer for you. Reveal to me the ways you're calling me to do so, for your glory and your fame. Amen.

Day 29

Psalm 24:1–6

¹God claims the world as his!
　　Everything and everyone belongs to him!
²He's the One who pushed back oceans
　　to let the dry ground appear,
　　planting firm foundations for the earth.
³Who, then, ascends into the presence of the Lord?
　　And who has the privilege of entering into
　　　　God's Holy Place?
⁴Those who are clean—whose works and ways are pure,
　　whose hearts are true and sealed by the truth,
　　those who never deceive, whose words are sure.
⁵They will receive the Lord's blessing
　　and righteousness given by the Savior-God.
⁶They will stand before God,
　　for they seek the pleasure of God's face,
　　　　the God of Jacob.

Pause in his presence

Lord, Give Me Clean Hands
and a Pure Heart!

*A*s Christians there are two things to consider with regards to this psalm:

First, positionally we have already been made clean and pure by the sacrificial blood of Christ. That's why Hebrews declares we can come before God's throne of grace with confidence to receive grace and mercy in our times of need.

Yet, we're not to come on our own terms; we need to come to God on his terms. Psalm 24 outlines those terms.

At the start, Yahweh is declared the exclusive King of creation, because, after all, "Everything and everyone belongs to him!" He separated the waters so that land could appear; he firmly planted the foundations of the earth. In light of God's total sovereignty, it makes total sense to ask the question the psalmist asks: "Who, then, ascends into the presence of the Lord? And who has the privilege of entering into God's holy place?"

In other words, who on earth can visit with this kind of God?

In many ways the answer to the question is thrown back in the questioner's court. Because, you see, we are invited to examine our own hearts and accept responsibility for what's in there.

When we come into God's presence—whether through personal prayer or corporate worship—do we come clean, with "works and ways" that are pure? Do we come with hearts that are "true and sealed by the truth"?

Many note that these two aspects of our personal standing before God—clean hands, pure heart—reflect two relationships: our relationship with others and God.

By "those who are clean" the psalmist is probably referring to the way we treat other people. In the original Hebrew it's literally "the one who has clean hands"—innocent people have clean hands not covered in the blood of others.

In the second phrase—"Whose hearts are true and sealed by the truth"—the psalmist is probably drawing our attention to the Jewish Shema, which called on Israel to love the Lord their God with their whole heart. There is a purity, a truthfulness about our inner being when we're loving God fully.

We prepare ourselves for entering into God's presence, then, when we do what Jesus directed us to do: "Love the Lord your God with every passion of your heart, with all the energy of your being, and with every thought that is within you! ... You must love your friend in the same way you love yourself" (Matthew 22:37, 39).

Perhaps this is why the ancient spiritual practice of the Daily Office begins each session with this confession:

Most merciful God,
I confess that I have sinned against you

in thought, word, and deed,
by what I have done,
and by what I have left undone.
I have not loved you with my whole heart;
I have not loved my neighbor as myself.
I am truly sorry and I humbly repent.
For the sake of your Son Jesus Christ,
have mercy on me and forgive me;
that I may delight in your will,
and walk in your ways,
to the glory of your Name. Amen.*

Notice how this prayer acknowledges one's sins against both God and neighbor, just like the psalmist. Both recognize that until we've repented of the sins we've committed against God and others, we can't ascend into the Lord's presence.

Yet when we do, what's waiting for us is simply amazing: the Lord's blessings for our every life and a right standing from our mighty Deliverer!

Positionally we have been cleansed, purified, and made right with God. But *personally* we are called to take stock and take responsibility.

So, then, how are you coming to the Lord when you pray and worship? Are you coming on God's terms, clean and pure, or yours? Ask the Holy Spirit to show you anything that hinders you from standing fully before him.

---

* *The Book of Common Prayer* (New York: Seabury Press, 1977).

Lenten Prayer

Lord Jesus Christ, Son of God, have mercy on me!
Give me clean hands; give me a pure heart, so that
I may ascend into your presence and worship you
unhindered. Amen.

Day 30

Luke 13:1–9

[1]Some of those present informed Jesus that Pilate had slaughtered some Galilean Jews while they were offering sacrifices at the temple, mixing their blood with the sacrifices they were offering.

[2]Jesus turned and asked the crowd, "Do you believe that the slaughtered Galileans were the worst sinners of all the Galileans? [3]No, they weren't! So listen to me. Unless you all repent, you will perish as they did. [4]Or what about the eighteen who perished when the tower of Siloam fell upon them? Do you really think that they were more guilty than all of the others in Jerusalem? [5]No, they weren't. But unless you repent, you will all eternally perish, just as they did."

[6]Then Jesus told them this parable: "There was a man who planted a fig tree in his orchard. But when he came to gather fruit from his tree he found none, for it was barren and had no fruit. [7]So he said to his gardener, 'For the last three years I've come to gather figs from my tree but it remains fruitless. What a waste! Go ahead and cut it down!'

[8]"But the gardener said, 'Sir, we should leave it one more year. Let me fertilize and cultivate it, then let's see if it will produce fruit. [9]If it doesn't bear fruit by next year, we'll cut it down.'"

The Parable of the Fig Tree and Lumberjack

*S*ometimes we can get it in our head that we're spiritually safe because we're religiously in.

We've prayed the "sinner's prayer," we read our Bible every day, we pray, we go to church every Sunday—twice even. So that must make us safe, right? Because we're insiders, we're good with God.

Maybe.

While these are all good things, sometimes they can foster a certain kind of religious attitude and blind us to a deeper need.

It's this attitude that Jesus confronts in today's reading, while also issuing a warning.

One day while Jesus was teaching, he was told some Galilean Jews were slaughtered by the regional governor, Pilate, who had a habit of doing such things. We're not told why Jesus was given this news, but his response makes one think it was because some thought these victims must have been particularly wretched sinners to suffer such a fate.

Instead of shaking his fist at Rome for committing such an act against his people, Jesus uses it as an object lesson, turning the tables on Israel!

Of all the people who should have been spiritually safe

because they were religiously *in*, it should have been Israel. After all, they were the people of God! Yet Jesus wants to pierce Israel's false sense of security, so he tells them a story about a farmer who planted a fig tree.

As the story goes, when it came time for the harvest, Mr. Fig Farmer went to gather the fruit off his tree, "yet it was barren and had no fruit"—apparently for three years running!

Understandably, Mr. Fig Farmer didn't want to waste any more time and water on his fruitless plant, so he ordered his gardener to cut it down.

His gardener, however, had a different idea. He made a deal with Mr. Fig Farmer: leave it for one more year to fertilize and cultivate it some more to see if it will produce fruit, then we'll chop it if it doesn't produce!

What is Jesus getting at?

Interestingly, fig trees are often used in the Hebrew Scriptures in connection with Israel. And barren or unproductive plants often symbolize the unfaithful nation of Israel or individual people. Finally, the image of cutting down a tree is connected to judgment.

Jesus was issuing his people a warning—and to all people really: You may think you're *in*, that you're safe, but you need to repent and produce fruit. Not tomorrow or down the road—today!

One person put it like this: If John said, "Repent, judgment is here!" Jesus is saying, "There's still time, but not much time, so repent!"

You see, the Jewish people were sitting in the comfort of their chosenness and religious rituals. Yet they weren't producing fruit—going on the three years or so of Jesus' ministry! So he has a message for them:

Like Mr. Fig Farmer, God requires fruit from each of his children, which is the result of a truly repentant heart. No amount of prayers, Bible reading, or church attendance can make you *safe*.

In Galatians 5:22–23, Paul reminds us of the kind of fruit the Bible says God requires of us: love that is revealed through joy, peace, patience, kindness, a life of virtue, gentleness, and strength of spirit.

This isn't meant to make you feel bad about how much you're failing. Instead, it's meant to remind us what Jesus reminded his people:

First, God's mercy is long and patient. He's like Mr. Fig Farmer: willing to wait for people to confess and repent of their sins.

But we also learn that a time will come when he will take action: he will cut down the trees that bear no fruit.

There's no way around it: God expects people to repent and his people to produce fruit in response to his grace and mercy. So, fig tree, how's your fruit? In what areas above do you need the Holy Spirit to do some tilling, pruning, and fertilizing in order to gather a bountiful harvest?

Lenten Prayer

Father, I confess I have sinned against you in thought, word, and deed; I have not loved you with my whole heart; and I have not loved my neighbor as myself. I am truly sorry and I humbly repent. Please forgive me and produce within me a bountiful harvest of sound character and spiritual fruit. Amen.

Day 31

Luke 13:22–27

²²Jesus ministered in one town and village after another, teaching the people as he made his way toward Jerusalem. ²³A bystander asked him, "Lord, will only a few have eternal life?"

Jesus said to the crowd, ²⁴"There is a great cost for anyone to enter through the narrow doorway to the kingdom of God. I tell you, there will be many who will want to enter but won't be able to. ²⁵For once the head of the house has shut and locked the door, it will be too late. Even if you stand outside knocking, begging to enter, and saying, 'Lord, Lord, open the door for us,' he will say to you, 'I don't know who you are. You are not a part of my family.'

²⁶"Then you will reply, 'But Lord, we dined with you and walked with you as you taught us.' ²⁷And he will reply, 'Don't you understand? I don't know who you are, for you are not a part of my family. You cannot enter in. Now, go away from me! For you are all disloyal to me and do evil.'"

Have You Entered the Narrow Doorway?

*T*here is this cave system in Kentucky called Mammoth Caves that perfectly illustrates what Jesus is talking about today. It's this massive network of caves that Native Americans and explorers apparently used for shelter and communal living. Two favorite sections are what they call Tall Man's Misery and Fat Man's Misery. You can probably tell what these experiences are like by their names!

In Tall Man's Misery there's this section that's way short. You have to stoop down and almost crawl through it to reach the other side. Fat Man's Misery is really narrow. You gotta suck it in and push on through. Neither are for the claustrophobic!

Have you ever noticed that following Jesus and his way isn't for the claustrophobic, either?

It is demanding and it is work. Often it's uncomfortable and downright difficult to do what Jesus calls us to do. And let's be honest: Sometimes it's no fun, either!

And yet, Jesus calls us to choose the narrow doorway in order to receive eternal life. It's a choice he posed during his famous Sermon on the Mount, too, when he taught:

Come to God through the narrow gate because the wide gate and broad path is the way that leads to destruction—nearly everyone chooses that crowded road! The narrow gate and the difficult way leads to eternal life—so few even find it!"

Now, on his way to Jerusalem in response to a question about receiving God's rescue, he says the same thing: Enter through the narrow doorway, or not, because one day it will be too late.

But what does it mean to *enter*, and what is this doorway we're supposed to go through?

Actually, what we discover is that the gate isn't a *what*, but a *who*! In John 10:7–9 Jesus insists *he* is the doorway:

> I speak to you eternal truth: I am the Gate for the flock. All those who broke in before me are thieves who came to steal, but the sheep never listened to them. I am the Gateway. To enter through me is to experience life, freedom, and satisfaction.

Through him and in him is life—the kind of life we all want, the kind of life God intends for us all. All other religious teachers and ways of living are false. Jesus is the way to God and his kingdom realm.

Yet, it's a narrow doorway, a small gate—one that's a struggle to enter through, rather than a stroll.

Following Jesus takes work. It requires that we stoop down, humble ourselves in repentance by turning away from our sin. It demands we forsake all other hope except him, to respond to his jealousy over us by giving ourselves to him completely.

Yet here is Jesus, calling us to make a decision. An uncompromising, life-altering, permanent, ongoing choice to follow Him by listening to his words and then obeying them.

Folks, there's no way around it: Jesus says choose my way or your way. The invitation to enter is given to everyone. The means of entering into God's saving rest has been accomplished through Jesus' death and resurrection. Now all that's left is for you to enter.

Have you? Will you?

Lenten Prayer

Jesus, thank you for suffering and sacrificing yourself on my behalf so that the door could be opened and the invitation sent for me to enter God's saving life! Today I hear that call and choose to enter, one step at a time.

Day 32

Luke 14:28-35

[27]And anyone who comes to me must be willing to share my cross and experience it as his own, or he cannot be considered to be my disciple. [28]So don't follow me without considering what it will cost you. For who would construct a house before first sitting down to estimate the cost to complete it? [29]Otherwise he may lay the foundation and not be able to finish. The neighbors will ridicule him, saying, [30]'Look at him! He started to build but couldn't complete it!'

[31]"Have you ever heard of a commander who goes out to war without first sitting down with strategic planning to determine the strength of his army to win the war against a stronger opponent? [32]If he knows he doesn't stand a chance of winning the war, the wise commander will send out delegates to ask for the terms of peace. [33]Likewise, unless you surrender all to me, giving up all you possess, you cannot be one of my disciples.

[34]"Salt is good for seasoning. But if salt were to lose its flavor, how could it ever be restored? [35]It will never be useful again, not even fit for the soil or the manure pile! If you have ears opened by the Spirit, then hear the meaning of what I have said and apply it to yourselves."

Count the Cost
of Discipleship

*D*ietrich Bonhoeffer is a modern hero of the faith. He passionately and fearlessly continued proclaiming the gospel and the lordship of Christ in the face of Nazi Germany—to the point of imprisonment and execution.

During this season Bonhoeffer penned one the most important books on the Christian life, *The Cost of Discipleship*. It has become a classic for understanding what it truly means to follow Jesus.

For Bonhoeffer, grace sat at the heart of discipleship, yet it wasn't cheap. Consider how he framed such a cost:

Costly grace is the gospel which must be sought again and again and again, the gift which must be asked for, the door at which a man must knock. Such grace is costly because it calls us to follow, and it is grace because it calls us to follow Jesus Christ. It is costly because it costs a man his life, and it is grace because it gives a man the only true life. It is costly because it condemns sin, and grace because it justifies the sinner. Above all, it is costly because it cost God the life of his Son: 'Ye were bought at a price', and what has cost God much cannot be cheap for us. Above all, it is grace because God did not reckon his Son too dear a price to pay for our life, but delivered him up for us. Costly grace is the Incarnation of God.*

Jesus seems to say the same thing in today's reading. He is inviting us to count the cost of following him—of giving every ounce of our life to his lordship. Because, friend, there is a cost—in the same way it costs a builder to build a tower or a king to go to war.

Who would begin a massive building project—say, the renovation of a family room—without figuring out whether he or she had the resources to accomplish the task? What ruler would consider going out to challenge an attacking king without analyzing whether it was better to fight and win, or surrender at the outset?

No one! And that's the point Jesus is making.

Why would anyone consider being a disciple without first assessing the impact such a following would have on one's life? It would be just as foolish!

Following Jesus changes our relationship with everything else in the world: allegiances to family and friends shift; discipleship requires a willingness to die; there is no room for self-centeredness; our lives are no longer our own.

You may protest that this sounds like super Christianity! Sort of…and yet, there are not two levels within the Christian faith—as if there were some who could be really committed,

---

* Dietrich Bonhoeffer, *The Cost of Discipleship* (New York: Touchstone, 1959), 45.

while others less so because of other attachments. No way! You're either following Christ, or you're not.

If Bonhoeffer were alive today he would be aghast at the "easy believism" that often marks Western Christianity— especially the American variety. After all, the gift of grace we experience cost a Man his life! "'Ye were bought at a price,'" Bonhoeffer reminds us, "and what has cost God much cannot be cheap for us."

Those are hard words, but necessary words. Because on our journey toward the cross this Lenten season, we need to take stock in whether we have cheapened God's gift to us. Jesus paid the ultimate consequence for our rebellion against God— suffering the most horrible death imagined by mankind.

So should we, whatever those consequences may be.

Bonhoeffer is right: "Grace at a low cost…brings neither help nor freedom."[*]

So how does it look in your life to "[consider] what it will cost you" to follow Jesus with every aspect of your life? (Luke 14:28).

Lenten Prayer

Father, I realize the cost you paid to give me the gift of your grace: the life of your Son. I don't want to ever cheapen this gift, so may I count the costs each day of what it means to follow Christ wholeheartedly!

---

[*] Greg Ligon, *Bonhoeffer's the Cost of Discipleship* (Nashville, TN: Broadman & Holman Publishers, 1999), 14

Day 33

Luke 16:1–7

¹Many dishonest tax collectors and other notorious sinners often gathered around to listen as Jesus taught the people. ²This raised concerns with the Jewish religious leaders and experts of the law. Indignant, they grumbled and complained, saying, "Look at how this man associates with all these notorious sinners and welcomes them all to come to him!"

³In response, Jesus gave them this illustration:

⁴⁻⁵"There once was a shepherd with a hundred lambs, but one of his lambs wandered away and was lost. So the shepherd left the ninety-nine lambs out in the open field and searched in the wilderness for that one lost lamb. He didn't stop until he finally found it. With exuberant joy he raised it up and placed it on his shoulders, carrying it back with cheerful delight! ⁶Returning home, he called all his friends and neighbors together and said, 'Let's have a party! Come and celebrate with me the return of my lost lamb. It wandered away, but I found it and brought it home.'"

⁷Jesus continued, "In the same way, there will be a glorious celebration in heaven over the rescue of one lost sinner who repents, comes back home, and returns to the fold—more so than for all the righteous people who never strayed away."

You Matter to God!

*I*f you've ever lost something, you know how absolutely *frustrating* it can be trying to find it again.

You set your wedding ring down, because you don't want it to get dirty or scuffed up while working—and *poof!* it goes missing. Or you set your keys down in a rush coming home, and they vanish into thin air. You swear you remember putting your paycheck in your pants pocket, yet suddenly it's gone.

Once you realize it's missing, the pursuit is on: You spend hours turning your home upside down, or you retrace your footsteps—driving all over town if you must!

Why do we go to such lengths to find the things we lose?

Because they matter to us! They're valuable, they have great worth. We'd go to the ends of the earth to seek the lost thing in order to find and rescue it.

Do you realize that's what God is like?

In our above reading we see that God is like a shepherd who seeks the one lost sheep in order to save it. God relentlessly pursues every one of us in order to rescue us and put us back together again—all because we're valuable; we have great worth; we matter to God!

Leading to this spiritual story, we are told tax collectors and sinners were flocking to Jesus. They represent the people who are far from God who need to be saved. They're also like that ring, set of keys, and missing paycheck—valuable, of great worth; they matter to God!

And so Jesus sought them out and shared a meal with them, which was huge. In his day, if you broke bread with someone, you were saying to them "You are valuable. I accept you. Your relationship matters to me."

From the looks of it Jesus did this often. He regularly ate with tax collectors and sinners, cultivated relationships with them, valued them—which meant he *accepted* them; they mattered to him!

The same is true of you: You matter to God!

Throughout the Bible people are often compared to sheep! In our story one lone sheep wandered off somewhere. The shepherd still had ninety-nine left over, but he did what any good shepherd would do: he left them to go find the one that was lost. Even though he still had ninety-nine to use for wool or food, he dropped everything to find this one.

Without the shepherd's help this lost sheep would not have found its way back to the flock. And the shepherd stopped at nothing to make sure it did. When he did finally find the sheep he carried it back on his shoulders, rejoicing—he even invited the whole community to join in the celebration!

One of the things that's fascinating about this story is how the sheep was *lost*—not that it wandered off. Something has happened to it. And then by his own desire the shepherd sought this lost sheep—without it first repenting of wandering away!

For Jesus' audience, the Pharisees, this would have been crazy! For them repentance was the very first thing required for acceptance. It was a condition for God's grace.

Not for Jesus. This story reminds us that for him, grace is what comes first. It is by his grace that God pursues us first, because we matter to him! It's only afterwards that we respond with repentance.

Jesus connects this earthly episode of the lost sheep to a heavenly one of the lost sinner who is found. He is basically telling the Pharisees "I seek the lost for God. This is who I am, this is what I do. I am like a shepherd who relentlessly searches in order to save, because people are valuable. They're of great worth. They matter to me!"

And if we celebrate when we find something we've lost of value—car keys or a wedding ring—just think how much more God celebrated when he found and rescued you!

Lenten Prayer

Heavenly Father, I am humbled that you find me valuable and of great worth—that I matter to you! At the start of each day remind me of the lengths that you went to find and rescue me, especially when I'm tempted to turn away from you. Amen.

Day 34

Luke: 19:1–10

¹⁻³In the city of Jericho there lived a very wealthy man named Zacchaeus, who was the supervisor over all the tax collectors. As Jesus made his way through the city, Zacchaeus was eager to see Jesus. He kept trying to get a look at him, but the crowd around Jesus was massive. Zacchaeus was a very short man and couldn't see over the heads of the people. ⁴So he ran on ahead of everyone and climbed up a blossoming fig tree so he could get a glimpse of Jesus as he passed by.

⁵When Jesus got to that place, he looked up into the tree and said, "Zacchaeus, hurry on down, for I am appointed to stay at your house today!"

⁶So he scurried down the tree and came face-to-face with Jesus.

⁷As Jesus left to go with Zacchaeus, many in the crowd complained, "Look at this! Of all the people to have dinner with, he's going to eat in the house of a crook."

⁸Zacchaeus joyously welcomed Jesus and was amazed over Jesus' gracious visit to his home. Zacchaeus stood in front of the Lord and said, "Half of all that I own I will give to the poor. And Lord, if I have cheated anyone, I promise to pay back four times as much as I stole."

⁹⁻¹⁰Jesus said to him, "This shows that today life has come to you and your household, for you are a true son of Abraham. The Son of Man has come to seek out and to give life to those who are lost."

Do Whatever It Takes for Jesus

*W*as there anything that you just *had* to have, and did whatever it took to get it or experience it?

Maybe your favorite singer was coming to town, so you stood in line all day to get tickets. Or maybe there was that *perfect* gift on sale on Black Friday, so you camped outside the department store to get it. Perhaps your friends were going to someplace warm for Spring break, so you saved every paycheck so you could join in the fun.

In today's reading we've got a story about a man who encountered Jesus, and when he did, he did whatever it took to follow him and experience his life.

During the latter part of his ministry, Jesus was heading toward Jerusalem. On the way he made a pit stop in Jericho. Like everywhere Jesus went, the crowds came out to see him—especially this one guy, Zacchaeus. He was a rich and powerful man, a tax collector.

In those days tax collectors were sort of like a mob boss.

The Roman government outsourced tax collection to these people. Rome sold the receipts of what was owed to the highest bidder—as if the IRS sold all of the taxes your city owned to a group of collectors. After the bidding war the tax collectors had to go out and recoup what *they* had just paid Rome—now Roman citizens owed *them*.

As you can imagine it was totally corrupt, mob-style. Tax collectors often cheated people out of their taxes, so they were viewed as wretched sinners.

That's this guy, and apparently he had heard about Jesus and wanted to get a glimpse of him—maybe because he heard stories about his compassion on people like him, that he dined with tax collectors and sinners.

But there was only one problem—he was too short! So when Jesus came through town Zacchaeus ran over and shimmied up a tree so he could get a glimpse of Jesus.

Which is sort of interesting, if you think about it. This guy had it all: lots of money, a fair amount of power, probably a degree of pleasure, too. Yet here he is, doing everything he can to encounter this man Jesus.

As he makes his way through Jericho, Jesus spots Zacchaeus hanging in the fig tree and calls him down. Actually, it was more than that: Jesus invited himself over to the man's house—invited himself into this man's life, ready or not.

And how does Zacchaeus respond? First, he scurried down the tree as fast as he could, then he rejoiced, and *then* he called Jesus Lord—he submitted to him as King by giving up his stuff to serve the poor, paying back his evil fourfold!

Zacchaeus surrendered his life completely to Jesus as king, and look at the result:

Jesus said to him, "This shows that today life has come to you and your household, for you are a true son of Abraham. The Son of Man has come to seek out and to give life to those who are lost."

A lot of people make this passage out to be about money, that in order to make it to heaven you need to take a vow of poverty. If that's the case then even Zacchaeus wouldn't have made it; he only donated half of his money!

This story isn't about giving money away, but giving our *life* away, handing over our own agenda, desires, demands—all of it—to Jesus.

Not many of us are rich, but the one thing we have in common with Zacchaeus is our life—what we're doing with it, who we're following with it.

What would it look like, right now, to do whatever it takes to experience Jesus and follow him as King?

Lenten Prayer

Jesus, I want to live my life as Zacchaeus: wholly abandoned to you in every way, doing whatever it takes to experience you and your life. Help me to follow you by giving my life away. Amen.

Day 35

Psalm 22:1–8

¹God, my God!

Why would you abandon me now?

²Why do you remain distant,

refusing to answer my tearful cries in the day

and my desperate cries for your help in the night?

I can't stop sobbing.

Where are you, my God?

³Yet, I know that you are most holy; it's indisputable.

You are God-Enthroned, surrounded with songs,

living among the shouts of praise of your princely people.

⁴Our fathers' faith was in you—

through the generations they trusted and believed in you

and you came through.

⁵Every time they cried out to you in their despair,

you were faithful to deliver them;

you didn't disappoint them.

⁶But look at me now; I am like a woeful worm,

crushed, and I'm bleeding crimson.

I don't even look like a man anymore.

I've been abused, despised, and scorned by everyone!

⁷Mocked by their jeers, despised with their sneers—
> as all the people poke fun at me, spitting their insults.

⁸Saying, "Is this the one who trusted in God?
> Is this the one who claims God is pleased with him?
> Now let's see if your God will come to your rescue!
> We'll just see how much he delights in you!"

Where Are You, My God?

*P*erhaps you've asked such a question yourself: "My God, where are you?"

You lost your job and are staring down the barrel of a past-due mortgage payment, dental bills, tuition for your child, and next week's grocery list. You watch on the news as another natural disaster wipes a foreign village off the map. That pain in your back turns out to be much more than sore muscles.

And you wonder what this psalmist wondered: "God, where on earth are you?"

Did you know Jesus asked his heavenly Father the same question? "My God, My God," Jesus said from the cross, "why have you left me helpless?" (Matthew 27:46).

When Jesus quoted these words from Psalm 22 while hanging on those beams of execution, he was identifying himself not only as the One David wrote about in this psalm, but also with David himself—with all of us, really, who have felt abandoned and left helpless by God. It is a breathtaking portrayal of what Jesus endured through his suffering for us, his identification with us.

While it's not stated in the crucifixion narrative, I wonder if Jesus recited the rest of this psalm silently in his head? He would have learned it and perhaps memorized it as a boy—probably sung it, too, in the synagogue along with the rest of his people as a cry to Yahweh for help.

And now he's quoting it while hanging on the cross and looking out at those for whom he was suffering, bleeding, and dying.

It's striking how closely the description of the psalmist fits Jesus' own situation:

> But look at me now; I am like a woeful worm,
> crushed, and I'm bleeding crimson.
> I don't even look like a man anymore.
> I've been abused, despised, and scorned by everyone!

After the abuse, suffering, and trauma from the crucifixion, Jesus would have been unrecognizable—he wouldn't have even looked like a man anymore! The prophet Isaiah anticipated that the Anointed One would be "crushed for our sins," and it would be by those crimson-gushing wounds we would be healed. (See Isaiah 53.)

Isaiah also prophesied the Messiah would be "despised

and rejected" by his people. To add insult to injury, Jesus had to endure the jeers and sneers of the crowd of Jewish onlookers who had come to Jerusalem for Passover, probably echoing the accusations of those who mocked the psalmist:

"Is this the one who trusted in God?
Is this the one who claims God is pleased with him?
Now let's see if your God will come to your rescue!
We'll just see how much he delights in you!"

Imagine what was going through Jesus' mind as he hung listening to words very similar to these. Perhaps he chose to meditate on what else the psalmist declared in between these two stanzas:

Yet, I know that you are most holy; it's indisputable.
You are God-Enthroned, surrounded with songs,
living among the shouts of praise of your princely people.
Our fathers' faith was in you—
through the generations they trusted and believed in you
and you came through.
Every time they cried out to you in their despair,
you were faithful to deliver them;
you didn't disappoint them.

The author of Hebrews reminds us that Jesus "pleaded with God, praying with passion and with tearful agony that God would spare him from death"—prayers that perhaps you yourself have prayed. The writer goes on to say that because of Christ's "perfect devotion"—a devotion that extended even to the cross—"his prayer was answered and he was delivered" (Hebrews 5:7).

The next time you are suffering and feel abandoned by God, remember that Jesus did, too. And yet, he wasn't; neither are you!

God is still faithful, he still doesn't disappoint.

Lenten Prayer

Almighty God, whose most dear Son went not up to joy but first he suffered pain, and entered not into glory before he was crucified: Mercifully grant that we, walking in the way of the cross, may find it none other than the way of life and peace; through Jesus Christ your Son our Lord, who lives and reigns with you and the Holy Spirit, one God, for ever and ever. Amen.*

---

* *The Book of Common Prayer* (New York: Seabury Press, 1977).

Day 36

John 12:23–26

²³He replied to them, "Now is the time for the Son of Man to be glorified. ²⁴Let me make this clear: A single grain of wheat will never be more than a single grain of wheat unless it drops into the ground and dies. Because then it sprouts and produces a great harvest of wheat—all because one grain died.

²⁵"The person who loves his life and pampers himself will miss true life! But the one who detaches his life from this world and abandons himself to me, will find true life and enjoy it forever! ²⁶If you want to be my disciple, follow me and you will go where I am going. And if you truly follow me as my disciple, the Father will shower his favor upon your life.

Lose Your Life to Keep It

For the longest time, Burger King was known by "Have It Your Way." Then in 2014 they ditched their forty-year-old slogan in favor of the more personal "Be Your Own Way."

In news reports, a company representative for Burger King was quoted as saying that "[customers] can and should live how they want anytime. It's OK to not be perfect.… Self-expression is most important and it's our differences that make us individuals instead of robots."[*]

This updated corporate promise and attitude is similar to other well-known advertising slogans: Sprite's "Obey Your Thirst" and Taco Bell's "Live Más"—live more.

Notice a theme here? These taglines aren't just corporate slogans; they're our world's slogans!

Whether through movies and TV shows, celebrities and artists, at every opportunity our culture urges us to love ourselves and advance our life at all costs. As modern people we believe that in order to truly live, we must hold onto our life by asserting our desires and interests, rights and agenda.

There's only one problem:

It's not true!

Jesus makes this perfectly clear one day on his way to the cross. The time was growing near for him to suffer and die for the sins of the world. When he announced that the time was almost ripe for his glorification, he told a little parable to illustrate what he was about to do:

"A single grain of wheat," Jesus said, "will never be more than a single grain of wheat unless it drops into the ground

---

[*] James Tonkowich, "Calvin, Aquinas and a Whopper with Cheese," accessed November, 8, 2015, http://www.christianheadlines.com /columnists/james-tonkowich/calvin-aquinas-and-a-whopper-with -cheese.html.

and dies. Because then it sprouts and produces a great harvest of wheat—all because one grain died."

Makes sense, right? In order for farmers to reap a bountiful harvest of wheat, a single grain must be planted in the ground. Instead of living on in baked goods around the world, the grain appears to suffer some sort of death.

Except Jesus says the exact opposite: The grain's "death" is actually the first step on its way toward life! It's only when the grain abandons itself to the ground that it can be fruitful.

In other words: death equals life!

Death equals life? Death *leads* to life? That's crazy talk! In our world, death equals death! Dying to self is thought of as a death, and holding onto ourselves is life. We think that we are actually losing something, that we are harming ourselves by denying ourselves.

But that's a lie! According to Jesus, in order to find life you must lose it; you must lose your life to keep it.

These slogans from Burger King, Sprite, and Taco Bell are diametrically opposed Jesus' way, which insists: "The person who loves his life and pampers himself will miss true life! But the one who detaches his life from this world and abandons himself to me will find true life and enjoy it forever!"

That's the point of Jesus' little parable about the grain. Death is exactly what's necessary for a fruitful life. And what looks like the grain's demise is actually the first step in an eventual bounty of life.

Same for Jesus: His resurrection-fruit came only after he suffered and died.

And the same is true for each of us. In order for us to find and experience true life—the kind of life that God offers us all—we must do the opposite of what our culture tells us to do.

So how would it look, right now, for you to detach your life from this world and abandon yourself to Christ alone?

Lenten Prayer

O God, by the passion of your blessed Son you made an instrument of shameful death to be for us the means of life: Help us to understand the glory of the cross of Christ, that we may gladly give our whole lives for the sake of your Son our Savior Jesus Christ, who lives and reigns with you and the Holy Spirit, one God, for ever and ever. Amen.*

---

* *The Book of Common Prayer* (New York: Seabury Press, 1977).

Day 37

John 12:27-36

²⁷"Even though I am torn within, and my soul is in turmoil, I will not ask the Father to rescue me from this hour of trial. For I have come to fulfill my purpose —*to offer myself to God.* ²⁸So, Father, bring glory to your name!" Then suddenly a booming voice was heard from the sky, "I have glorified my name! And I will glorify it *through you* again!"

²⁹The audible voice of God startled the crowd standing nearby. Some thought it was only thunder, yet others said, "An angel just spoke to him!"

³⁰Then Jesus told them, "The voice you heard was not for my benefit, but for yours—*to help you believe.* ³¹From this moment on, everything in this world is about to change, for the ruler of this dark world will be overthrown. ³²*And I will do this* when I am lifted up off the ground and when I draw the hearts of people to gather them to me." ³³He said this to indicate that he would die by being lifted up on the cross.

³⁴People from the crowd spoke up and said, "Die? How could the Anointed One die? The Word of God says that the Anointed One will live with us forever, but you just said that the Son of Man must be lifted up from the earth. And who is this Son of Man anyway?"

³⁵Jesus replied, "You will have the light shining with you for only a little while longer. While you still have me, walk in the light, so that the darkness doesn't overtake you. For when you walk in the dark you have no idea where you're going. ³⁶So believe and cling to the light while I am with you, so that you will become children of light." After saying this, Jesus then entered into the crowd and hid himself from them.

Father, Glorify Your Name!

Sometimes the suffering we experience in this life seems entirely pointless, purposeless, and random—like, what's the point of such experiences?

From cancer to car wrecks, fires to foreclosures, depression to death itself, it seems preposterous to find a silver lining, some sort of reason for such hardship. In fact, some skeptics of Christianity have even wondered why Jesus had to suffer and die at all—accusing God of "divine child abuse."

Remarkably, what Christ's own experience with suffering shows us is that we, like him, can accept joyfully the sufferings of the present time, being confident of the glory that will be revealed in and through them.

As we make our way to the cross during Holy Week through the gospel of John, we find Jesus praying to the

Father in agony. Here, he *is* deeply depressed; he is "torn within" and his soul "is in turmoil." Some of us can probably relate given our own experience with suffering.

Despite this agony, turmoil, and depression, however, Jesus is more resolved than ever to crawl up on those beams of execution as a sacrifice for your sins, my sins, and the sins of the entire world! Rather than praying for the removal of the cup, as he does in Gethsemane, Jesus prays, "Father, bring glory to your name!"

Because you see, that was the point of Christ's own suffering and sacrifice.

It's amazing when you think about it: by giving himself over in obedience to the Father's plan to rescue us from our sins—even through suffering and death—the Son ultimately honored and exalted the Father! Perhaps another way of wording Christ's prayer is this: "Father, may your Son be crucified!"

What a prayer to pray! In it we see Jesus' complete surrender and obedience to the will of his Father. Jesus is saying "May I suffer and experience the agony and turmoil of the cross, all for your fame, your honor—Your glory!"

In response, the Father told everyone around he had already been honored throughout Jesus' obedient life and ministry, yet his honor would reach greater heights through the cross: "Son, I have been honored and exalted throughout your life and ministry—and in a few days I will be so once more!"

And it was, precisely because Jesus was obedient to the Father's saving plan. As Jesus told the crowd: "Everything in this world is about to change" because of his suffering and death. The hour had dawned for two things to happen: both judgment and redemption. Judgment, "for the ruler of this dark world will be overthrown"; redemption, for Jesus would be "lifted off the ground" and he would "draw the hearts of people to gather them" to himself.

Not only did Jesus glorify the Father through obedience— he defeated Satan and saved humanity! So, you see, Jesus' sufferings weren't for nothing. Neither are ours.

When we experience hardship, is our impulse obedience? Is it to glorify and honor our heavenly Father's name in the midst of it?

Our suffering is never pointless, purposeless, and random. Paul reminds us that "every detail of our lives is continually woven together to fit into God's perfect plan of bringing what is good into our lives, for we are his lovers who have been invited to fulfill his designed purpose" (Romans 8:28). Ultimately, that purpose is the same purpose of Christ:

To bring God honor, to obey him, and glorify his name!

May we face suffering the same way Christ did: with unwavering obedience and honor of the One who weaves every detail of our lives together to bring us into our destiny!

Lenten Prayer

Lord God, whose blessed Son our Savior gave his body to be whipped and his face to be spit upon: Give us grace to accept joyfully the sufferings of the present time, confident of the glory that shall be revealed; through Jesus Christ your Son our Lord, who lives and reigns with you and the Holy Spirit, one God, for ever and ever. Amen. [*]

---

* *The Book of Common Prayer* (New York: Seabury Press, 1977).

Day 38

John 13:2–15, 34–35

²Before their evening meal had begun, the accuser had already planted betrayal into the heart of Judas Iscariot, the son of Simon.

³Now Jesus was fully aware that the Father had placed all things under his control, for he had come from God and was about to go back to be with him. ⁴So he got up from the meal and took off his outer robe, and took a towel and wrapped it around his waist. ⁵Then he poured water into a basin and began to wash the disciples' dirty feet and dry them with his towel.

⁶But when Jesus got to Simon Peter, he objected and said, "I can't let you wash my dirty feet—you're my Lord!"

⁷Jesus replied, "You don't understand yet the meaning of what I'm doing, but soon it will be clear to you."

⁸Peter looked at Jesus and said, "You'll never wash my dirty feet—never!"

"But Peter, if you don't allow me to wash your feet," Jesus responded, "then you will not be able to share life with me."

⁹So Peter the Rock said, "Lord, in that case, don't just wash my feet, wash my hands and my head too!"

¹⁰Jesus said to him, "You are already clean. You've been washed completely and you just need your feet to be cleansed—but that can't be said of all of you." For Jesus knew which one was about to betray him, ¹¹and that's why he told them that not all of them were clean.

¹²After washing their feet, he put his robe on and returned to his place at the table. "Do you understand what I just did?" Jesus said. ¹³"You've called me your teacher and lord, and you're right, for that's who I am. ¹⁴⁻¹⁵So if I'm your teacher and lord and have just washed your dirty feet, then you should follow the example that I've set for you and wash one another's dirty feet. Now do for each other what I have just done for you.

³⁴"So I give you now a new commandment: Love each other just as much as I have loved you. ³⁵For when you demonstrate the same love I have for you by loving one another, everyone will know that you're my true followers."

The Basin and the Towel

*T*oday we celebrate Maundy Thursday. No, not *Monday* Thursday. Maundy. The name comes from the Old French word *mande*, which comes from the Latin *mandatum novum*, meaning "new commandment." The day is associated with the new command Jesus gave his disciples shortly before the cross.

Here was the scene:

Jesus and the disciples have just sat down to enjoy what will be their final meal together. The disciples don't know it, but Jesus does. And he has something special in mind in order to teach an important lesson about how they are to live together—and also what's to come.

With his face set like flint toward the cross, and knowing who he was and what his mission was, he got up from the table, shed his clothes, wrapped a towel around his waist, stooped down, and started serving his disciples.

Wielding nothing more than a basin and a towel!

To fully understand what's going on here you need to understand something about the footwear of Jesus' day—or lack thereof. As you can imagine, they didn't have the same kind of fancy closed-toed shoes we have today. Back then they would have worn open-toed sandals, if anything at all. Over the course of the day they would have walked through lots of different things—dirt and dust, mud and stuff that looked like mud.

And all of that would have been caked on the feet of Jesus' disciples, in between their toes and underneath their toenails!

Yet here is Jesus, washing it off. With nothing more than a basin and a towel!

Now *that's* love!

Typically, this kind of task was left to either the housemaids or the woman of the house. The master or lord of the house, even men in general, would never have done such a thing. And yet, there is Jesus. Stooped down low, on the ground, with nothing on besides a large towel and armed with a bowl of water.

As you can imagine, the disciples are nearly choking on their meal once they see what Jesus is doing. Even Peter says, "Jesus, no way!"

So Jesus asks them, "Do you understand what I just did?" and then goes on to explain the significance of what just happened:

"You've called me your teacher and lord," he says "and you're right, for that's who I am. So if I'm your teacher and lord and have just washed your dirty feet, then you should follow the example that I've set for you and wash one another's dirty feet. Now do for each other what I have just done for you" (John 13:13–15).

Jesus said the disciples would soon understand the full extent of what he was doing. He was loving his friends with two ordinary elements: a basin full of water and a silk towel. Later he would love them and the world with two extraordinary elements: his very own body and blood.

After Jesus washes his friends' feet, they resumed the meal. At one point Jesus reached over and grabbed a loaf of bread and cup of wine, offering them as symbols of the body he would break open and blood he would shed to wash them completely clean.

He also gave them a new command that would demonstrate to the world the love Christ had and would demonstrate for them: "Love each other just as much as I have loved you."

Why? Because when we love others as Jesus first loved us "everyone will know that you're my true followers," as he said.

The basin and the towel; the body and blood. Both remind us how we are to live with each other in this world—a life of self-sacrifice.

Just like Jesus.

Lenten Prayer

Almighty Father, whose dear Son, on the night before he suffered, instituted the sacrament of his body and blood: Mercifully grant that we may receive it thankfully in remembrance of Jesus Christ our Lord, who in these holy mysteries gives us a pledge of eternal life; and who now lives and reigns with you and the Holy Spirit, one God, forever and ever. Amen.[*]

---

[*] *The Book of Common Prayer* (New York: Seabury Press, 1977).

Day 39

John 19:17-30

¹⁷Jesus carried his own cross out of the city to the place called "The Skull," which in Aramaic is Golgotha. ¹⁸And there they nailed him to the cross. He was crucified, along with two others, one on each side with Jesus in the middle. ¹⁹⁻²⁰Pilate had them post a sign over the cross, which was written in three languages—Aramaic, Latin, and Greek. Many of the people of Jerusalem read the sign, for he was crucified near the city. The sign stated: "Jesus of Nazareth, the King of the Jews."

²¹But the chief priests of the Jews said to Pilate, "You must change the sign! Don't let it say, 'King of the Jews,' but rather—'he claimed to be the King of the Jews!'" ²²Pilate responded, "What I have written will remain!"

²³Now when the soldiers crucified Jesus, they divided up his clothes into four shares, one for each of them. But his tunic was seamless, woven from the top to the bottom as a single garment. ²⁴So the soldiers said to each other, "Don't tear it—let's throw dice to see who gets it!" The soldiers did all of this not knowing they fulfilled the Scripture that says, "They divided my garments among them and gambled for my garment."

²⁵Miriam, Jesus' mother, was standing next to his cross, along with Miriam's sister, Miriam the wife of Clopas, and Miriam Magdalene. ²⁶So when Jesus looked down and saw the disciple he loved standing with her, he said, "Mother, look—John will be a son to you." ²⁷Then he said, "*John,* look—she will be a mother to you!" From that day on, John accepted Mary into his home *as one of his own family.*

²⁸Jesus knew that his mission was accomplished, and to fulfill the Scripture, Jesus said: "I am thirsty."

²⁹A jar of sour wine was sitting nearby, so they soaked a sponge with it and put it on the stalk of hyssop and raised it to his lips. ³⁰When he had sipped the sour wine, he said, "It is finished, my bride!" Then he bowed his head and surrendered his spirit to God.

It Is Finished!

We have arrived near the end of our forty-day Lenten march, and at the reason for that march in the first place: the suffering and sacrifice of Christ.

Because Lent is a season to consider and contemplate the gravity of what the cross entailed, I want to take you deep into this ancient practice to fully grasp what it was that Jesus experienced for the world—for you. The typical Christian painting depicting Christ's passion is a sanitary version of what really happened:

While crucifixion was widely practiced in the ancient world, it was the Romans who perfected the "art" of punishing someone by nailing or binding them to two beams placed at cross sections of each other, or simply a stake in the ground or tree.

This punishment was usually reserved for those who were a threat to the empire—for rebels and terrorists, for people Rome deemed "enemies of the state." Often the empire would crucify people and groups of people along public roads and at the city gates. They wanted the maximum amount of people to see what would happen to *them* if they took on Rome.

Crucifixion was *the* worst death imaginable at the time. A famous Roman politician, Cicero, called it a "most cruel and disgusting penalty," given how sadistic and barbaric the practice had become under Roman rule.

It often began with torture: Before crucifying someone, Roman guards would flog their victims with a device that had a wooden handle with long strips of leather coming out at the top. Attached were pieces of metal and hooks that would tear at the flesh of the victims. Destroying their backs. Ripping out their scalp or pieces of their face.

Jesus was flogged this way—and then beaten and spit upon and mocked.

Victims were typically forced carry their own crossbeam of execution. Once they reached the crucifixion, Jesus was placed on those beams—naked. He was completely exposed, adding to the humiliation and shame.

Then spikes, similar to those you might find laying on railroad tracks, were pounded into both of Jesus' wrists and one through both feet.

And then he waited—for the moment when it would happen.

While he waited he couldn't swat at the flies crawling over his wounds. He wouldn't have been able to hold his bodily waste. The heat would have been suffocating—over one hundred degrees. And because spikes tore through tendons and bones Jesus had to use his back muscles to support himself. He would also have had to push up on that single nail pounded through his feet. So Jesus had to alternate between supporting himself on the single nail and arching his back—just to continue to breathe, to stay alive.

For you and me and every person on the planet!

This, brothers and sisters, was Jesus' entire mission: to suffer in this way by sacrificing himself to pay the penalty of our acts of rebellion against God, in our place.

He paid the price for racism and child sex slavery and the Holocaust.

He paid the price for pornography and gossip and divorce.

He paid the price for warlords and soccer moms, pimps and stay-at-home dads.

He paid *your* price. In *your* place.

And when he did, when he bore the full weight of God's

wrath for all the sins committed by individuals and societies from ages past to ages future, he cried out those magnificent, beautiful, glorious words:

It is finished!

Lenten Prayer

Almighty God, we pray you graciously to behold this your family, for whom our Lord Jesus Christ was willing to be betrayed, and given into the hands of sinners, and to suffer death upon the cross; who now lives and reigns with you and the Holy Spirit, one God, forever and ever. Amen.[*]

---

[*] *The Book of Common Prayer* (New York: Seabury Press, 1977).

Day 40

John 19:38–42

³⁸After this, Joseph from the city of Ramah, who was a secret disciple of Jesus for fear of the Jewish authorities, asked Pilate if he could remove the body of Jesus. So Pilate granted him permission to remove the body from the cross. ³⁹Now Nicodemus, who had once come to Jesus privately at night, accompanied Joseph, and together they carried a significant amount of myrrh and aloes to the cross. ⁴⁰Then they took Jesus' body and wrapped it in strips of linen with the embalming spices according to the Jewish burial customs. ⁴¹Near the place where Jesus was crucified was a garden, and in the garden there was a new tomb where no one had yet been laid to rest. ⁴²And because the Sabbath was approaching, and the tomb was nearby, that's where they laid the body of Jesus.

A Day of Darkness...and Hope

We end this devotional the way we began it: In death.

At the beginning we contemplated our own eventual death, our mortality. And, while yesterday we celebrated Christ's death and all it means for you and me, at the end we contemplate the death of Christ. Yes, we know he has risen from the dead in full glory and splendor, but that will come tomorrow.

Today, though, we sit at the Lord's tomb. Jesus' body has been embalmed; it's been wrapped and laid to rest; the tomb has been sealed shut by the great stone.

And now we wait, called to sit and meditate on his passion and death, and on his descent into hell to rescue the dead, and await his resurrection with prayer and fasting.

We wait along with "Mary Magdalene and the other Marys, who watched all that took place" (Matthew 27:63) outside the tomb; we wait with others like Nicodemus, who first met Jesus early in his ministry.

Nicodemus' story is interesting, because John's gospel tells us that he was a Pharisee, one of the "separated ones" who were Jewish religious teachers. If you're familiar with Jesus' story, you know that the Pharisees had it in for Jesus. They were constantly after him, trying to trap him and discredit him.

There must have been something about Jesus that fascinated Nicodemus and piqued his interest, however, because John 3 reveals that one evening, under the cover of darkness, he sought Jesus out to better understand who he was and what he offered.

And then smack-dab in the middle of his story is this gem-of-a-revelation by Jesus:

"And just as Moses in the desert lifted up the brass replica of a snake on a pole *for all the people to see and be healed*, so the Son of Man is ready to be lifted up, so that those who truly believe in him will not perish but be given eternal life. For this is how much God loved the world—he gave his one and only, unique Son *as a gift*. So now everyone who believes in him will never perish but experience everlasting life." (John 3:14–16)

Of course, Jesus is speaking here of his death by being "lifted up" on the cross. In fact, Jesus reveals that God the Father gave the world his Son, Jesus, for the purpose of experiencing this "lifting up"—for the purpose of dying.

This is how much God loves the world; this is how much God loves you!

And it is when we believe in Christ's death on the cross for the payment of our sins and the defeat of death through his resurrection that we receive salvation and are made new!

It's clear from Nicodemus' story that he did believe. He wouldn't have risked being publicly seen with Jesus carrying around nearly seventy-five pounds of spices for his body if he didn't! Apparently, Nicodemus hadn't forgotten Jesus' sermon when they first met. He trusted in who Jesus was and what Jesus did. He was right there with Joseph caring for Christ's body and helping bury it.

You see, when we first met him, Nicodemus was eager for the hope of the kingdom realm of God (John 3:3). When we meet him again, he has found the King of that kingdom and prepared a burial fit for a king!

Yes, this day is a day of darkness, because it was a day of death. But the hopeful truth of Jesus' story is that he didn't stay that way.

And neither will you! For the same hopeful promise Jesus gave Nicodemus is the same one he has for you, too:

Everyone who believes in him will never perish but experience everlasting life. (John 3:16)

Lenten Prayer

*O God, Creator of heaven and earth: Grant that, as the crucified body of your dear Son was laid in the tomb and rested on this holy Sabbath, so we may await with him the coming of the third day, and rise with him to newness of life; who now lives and reigns with you and the Holy Spirit, one God, forever and ever. Amen.**

---

* *The Book of Common Prayer* (New York: Seabury Press, 1977).

About The Passion Translation

The Passion Translation Bible is a new, heart-level translation that expresses God's fiery heart of love to this generation, using Hebrew, Greek, and Aramaic manuscripts and merging the emotion and life-changing truth of God's Word.

God longs to have his Word expressed in every language in a way that unlocks the passion of his heart. The goal of this work is to trigger inside every reader an overwhelming response to the truth of the Bible, unfolding the deep mysteries of the Scriptures in the love language of God, the language of the heart.

If you are hungry for God and want to know him on a deeper level, The Passion Translation will help you encounter God's heart and discover what he has for your life.

For information about all books in The Passion Translation and future releases, please visit

thepassiontranslation.com

Encounter the Heart of God

This box set includes the following eight Passion Translation books:

Psalms: Poetry on Fire

Proverbs: Wisdom from Above

Song of Songs: Divine Romace

Matthew: Our Loving King

John: Eternal Love

Luke and Acts: To the Lovers of God

Hebrews and James: Faith Works

Letters from Heaven: From the Apostle Paul
(Galatians, Ephesians, Philippians, Colossians, I & II Timothy)

THE
PASSION
TRANSLATION

thepassiontranslation.com